MATLOU SELEPE

"Unforgiveness enslaves him who entertains it. It grabs it's victim and holds him tight until he suffocates."

The Releasing Power of Forgiveness

This publication contains the opinions and ideas of Scripture. It is intended to provide helpful and informative material on the subjects addressed in the publication. The author and publisher specifically disclaim all responsibility for any liability, loss or risk, personal or otherwise, which is incurred as a consequence, directly or indirectly, of the use and application of any of the contents of this book.

WORKBOOK PRESS LLC
187 E Warm Springs Rd,
Suite B285, Las Vegas, NV 89119, USA

Website: https://workbookpress.com/
Hotline: 1-888-818-4856
Email: admin@workbookpress.com

Ordering Information:
Quantity sales. Special discounts are available on quantity purchases by corporations, associations, and others.
For details, contact the publisher at the address above.

Library of Congress Control Number:
ISBN-13:   000-0-000000-00-0 (Paperback Version)
              000-0-000000-00-0 (Digital Version)

REV. DATE: 06/27/2022

The Releasing Power of Forgiveness

By

Apostle Matlou Selepe

Table of Contents

Part Three

Practical steps to remove huddles of unforgiveness

Part Four Testimony

Part Five
Conclusions

Introduction

One of the most effective weapons the kingdom of darkness has unleashed against human beings is unforgiveness. This weapon alone has the potential of bringing the entire human race to extinction. Christianity is centered around forgiveness, the belief that as we acknowledge our transgression before our Father in the name of His Son Jesus Christ our Lord, God forgives us unconditionally. This belief alone sets us on a path of peace and joy that surpasses human understanding which ultimately lead us into eternal communion with God the creator.

In fact, no human being can ever comprehend such a grace and mercy as this. But all this hangs on the fact that we as human beings, come to our senses and acknowledge that we are by nature children of wrath, not perfect, far from the saving grace of God. And having accepted this, ask forgiveness from God for all our transgressions, believing that as we confess to Him, His mercy covers us and the blood of Jesus Christ vaporize our sins, bringing us a new sense of hope of a better tomorrow. It is on this basis that God's mercy and grace remain sufficient for all of us.

However, it should be noted that unforgiveness on the other hand works hand in hand with deception and pride. Deception in particular, is very dangerous as the person being deceived cannot see that he is being deceived. Satan uses this loop hole to bring more thoughts as to confuse his victim. Once I was watching a boxing match on television, when Dingaan Thobela, three times world champion, commented that the boxers needed to throw as many punches as to confuse the judges. Upon analyzing this statement, I found it to be true to the spiritual warfare cases, more so the battle of the mind.

I came to realize that the enemy throws many thoughts to our minds and we end up being confused by all his lies and this opens up the door for deception which leads to pride, unless we move swiftly to bring these thoughts into captivity under the obedience of Jesus Christ our Lord and Savior. Pride when gaining enough ground is very difficult to remove. Pride says, I am right and you are wrong, you have started it and you don't deserve my forgiveness. Dr. Charles Stanley writes "We don't have a right to withhold forgiveness from anyone, and that certainly includes our friends" (In Touch Daily Devotional) 1.

Humanity has come under fierce attacks from the kingdom of darkness using unforgiveness as an effective weapon of human destruction. Many friendships have collapsed and some on the brink of collapse due to unforgiveness. The very gospel that saw Jesus our Lord descending from heaven to come on earth, that He may redeem human race. The very gospel that is being preached daily and prayed daily through the Lord's prayer, yet the same old weapon Satan our enemy so effectively uses.

There are many reasons that we can mention that causes unforgiveness and lead couples to divorce, family collapsing, brothers separating etc. and each of them are seemingly justifiable. But I want us to go and look at the biblical responsibilities of each person regarding forgiveness compared to unforgiveness. Christians are called to forgive each other in regardless of the extent of the hurt. Tony Wegerly wrote, *"It is not impossible for the hurting person to forgive because it releases peace and freedom"(2)*.

Throughout this book, we will explore what I call the major reasons why Christians ought to forgive unconditionally and hope that merciful Lord would use this book to bring you to that point where you can forgive at ease. I also pray that the Lord will use this book to release many of our people bound by the chains and shackles of bitterness which yields worms and death.

Special Acknowledgements

This book is dedicated to all brethren and couples in particular, who are struggling with the burden and yokes of unforgiveness. May the Lord of mercy use this book to bring light to the darkness of your struggles and be set free in the name of Jesus Christ our Lord and Savior!

"It shall come to pass in that day that his burden will be taken away from your shoulder, and his yoke from your neck, and the yoke will be destroyed because of the anointing oil" Isaiah 10:27.

Amen.

Remember always to *"Stand fast therefore in the liberty by which Christ has made us free, and do not be entangled again with a yoke of bondage"* Galatians 5:1.

Part One

Biblical Order

Of Dealing with

Forgiveness

Our battle is not against

blood and flesh

"For we do not wrestle against flesh *and blood, but against principalities, against powers, against the rulers of the darkness of this age, against spiritual hosts of wickedness in the heavenly places" Ephesians 6:12*

The bible records that when Lucifer was thrown out of heaven, he came down to the earth and the sea. The immediate warning to the inhabitants of these places was that woe would befall them as Satan comes with a great wrath knowing that his time is short (Revelation 12:12). Again, the scriptures warn us of his anger and the subsequence hatred towards the offspring of the woman whom he tried to kill but failed. This is how the bible recorded the accounts of this event.

"Now when the dragon (another name for Satan) saw that he had been cast to the earth, he persecuted the woman who gave birth to the male child. But the woman was given two wings of a great eagle, that she might fly into the wilderness to her place, where she is nourished for a time and times and a half a time, from the presence of the serpent. So, the serpent spewed water out of his mouth like a flood after the woman that he might cause her to be carried away by the flood. But the earth helped he woman, and the earth opened its mouth and swallowed up the flood which the dragon had spewed out of his mouth. And the dragon was enraged with the woman, **and he went to make war with the rest of her off-spring, who keep the**

commandments of God and have the testimony of Jesus Christ" *revelation 12:13-17.*

Verse 12 tells us that the enemy is having a great wrath and verse 17 repeats almost with the same tone, the wrath of the enemy. But the climax of this hatred is vented against the rest of her off-spring especially those who keep the commandments of God and have the testimony of Jesus Christ. This my friends refers to the born-again Christians who have the spirit of prophesy, for the testimony of Jesus Christ is the spirit of prophesy (Revelation 19:10). Now the apostle John in his first epistle guides us thus,

"By this you know the Spirit of God; every spirit that confesses that Jesus Christ has come in the flesh is of God" *1 John 4:2.*

To have the testimony of Jesus Christ is to confirm that He has come in the flesh and this affirmation can only be made by the sons and daughters of the kingdom whom Christ Himself has made them both kings and priests unto His God and Father who alone deserves the glory and the honor forever and ever (Revelation 1:6). No blood and flesh can reveal this mystery but the Holy Spirit of Truth (Matthew16:17). This then makes any person who profess Christianity a direct target and enemy number one of our ruthless opponent.

It is due to this formidable character of our enemy that the bible encourages us to walk in the Spirit at all times. We need to understand that Satan as a spirit cannot come into the world and begin to literally fights us. As a spirit being, he needs a body from which he can use as a base to unleash his wicked divisive spirits to the families and human race at large. And due to man's constant battle with his sinful fallen nature, he therefore becomes susceptible to satanic influence at times. But when we walk with conscious understanding that we have an enemy who is filled with a great wrath, we would become vigilant and radical in dealing with him. We need to always remember what Paul wrote to the church in Corinth,

"For though we walk in the flesh, we do not war according to the flesh. For our weapons of our warfare are not carnal but mighty in God for pulling down strongholds, casting down arguments and every high thing that exalts itself against the knowledge of God, bringing every thought into captivity to the obedience of Christ" 2 Corinthians 10:3-5.

We spoke of the mind as a sight on target by the forces of darkness and Paul here admonishes us to take captive every thought bringing it into captivity under the obedience of Jesus Christ. This is because if the mind is overcome, the battle is over. When Satan approached Eve in the garden, his first target was Eve's mind. He brought doubt to her through his question. *"Has God indeed said, „You shall not eat of every tree of the garden?" (Genesis 3:1).* Satan used the word indeed to bring doubt to her mind. He knew that she knows for sure that God gave them the instruction not to eat of the tree of knowledge of good and evil, but he did that purposefully to plant the seed of doubt. By accepting the doubt, the woman gave Satan an opportunity to further convince her of the benefits of eating from the tree. This is the reason why for the first time, she started looking at the fruit in a different light and the rest is history.

> *"So, when the woman so that the tree was good for food, that it was pleasant to the eyes, and a tree desirable to make on wise, she took of its fruit and ate". Genesis 3:6.*

By telling her the benefits of disobedience, that the tree would open her eyes and make her wise, he caused her to focus on herself other than fixing her eyes on God, the Father. This created the pride of self. It's all about me. We should not forget that he is a master of pride. The book of Job puts it this way, *"He beholds every high thing; he is king over all the children of pride" Job 41:34.* If Satan can manage to convince a spouse, he has the couple where he wants them, fighting against each other over unnecessary things. The same principle applies to brothers and sisters alike. It is on this basis that the bible encourages us to be kindly affectionate to one another with brotherly love, in honor giving preference to one another (Romans 12:10). Another verse says, *"Do not be overcome by evil, but overcome evil with good" Romans 12:21.* If the enemy manages to maneuver and conquer the man's mind, he will cause major havoc. The responsibility lies with us to acknowledge the spiritual warfare facing us and be ready to join forces to guard ourselves.

> *"Two are better than one, because they have a good reward for their labor...and a threefold cord is not quickly broken" Ecclesiastes 4:9&12.*

Gird the loins of your hearts, quicken yourselves and prepare for the war. Our enemy is formidable and ruthless but disarmed by our Lord Jesus Christ through whom our Father always leads us in triumph (1 Corinthians 15:57). We are guaranteed of the victory for Christ has made us more than conquerors (Romans 8:37) if we fix our eyes unto Him who is the author and the finisher of our faith (Hebrews 12:2). Our Father, the God of peace is ready to crush Satan under our feet shortly (Romans 16:20) if only we can let Him do it through us.

Satan's two most lethal weapons used against human race are accusation and deception. Through this, he is able to turn brother against brother without them having slightest idea of his involvement. The civil wars in Burundi, Rwanda, Sierra Leon and most recently in Kenya highlight this effective weapon the enemy uses against human beings. In all these countries, he managed to turn families and brothers against each other through deception. He is an unseen force behind all the quarrels, church breakups, wars and contentions in the world. Unless we arm ourselves with the truth of the word of God, we cannot be able to defeat him. Our brother can never be our enemy.

In fact, no blood and flesh can be our enemy. We have only one enemy, that very serpent of old, Satan and dragon. He is a spirit being operating spiritually with devastating consequences in the natural realm among humans. Satan is determined to cause conflicts among people and would stop at nothing to achieve his goal. If we can understand that this is a spiritual warfare and stop pointing fingers of blame against one another once things go wrong, we would go a long way in defeating this enemy. Blaming and fighting each other only plays in the hands of the enemy and strengthens his hand of deception over us.

Peter warns us that he is roaming around, looking for whom he can devour (1 Peter 5:8). This means, he would pounce on any slightest misunderstanding between people, binding them with his deceptive tentacles while laying heavy burdens and yokes of accusations upon them. If they lack discernment, he would drown them in the lake of bitterness and unforgiveness. The solution here is to walk in the Spirit so as to overcome the world through our faith in Christ Jesus while carnality plays in his outstretched hands. *"For we walk by faith, not by sight"* 2 *Corinthians 5:7.*

No man can ever win the spiritual warfare using the physical means; even so, for us to overcome the enemy, we need to resort to the spiritual weapons. As we remember that our battle is not against blood and flesh, let us therefore arm ourselves with the spiritual armory which is powerful through God for the pulling down of the strongholds. But if we lose sight of this and begin to walk by sight, we have already been defeated even before the battle begins.

One pastor said to me recently, a person becomes entangled in the spiritual warfare the minutes he becomes a born-again

Christian. This means immediately the light of the Truth shines in your heart, you are then marked for target by the kingdom of darkness. Your real battles begin. You are going to have to be vigilant in life and embrace the Truth of the Scriptures which are able to make you wise for salvation through faith which is in Christ Jesus (2Timothy 3:15). Our Lord Jesus is the True, the Way and the Life and through Him we have the victory over every scheme the enemy can conjure.

> *"These things I have spoken to you, that in Me you may have peace. In the world you will have tribulation; but be of good cheer, I have overcome the world" John 16:33.*

Furthermore, we know that our weapons of warfare are not carnal but mighty in God for the pulling down of the strongholds, casting down arguments and every high thing that exalts itself against the knowledge of God. Secondly, our faith is very critical in a spiritual warfare. We shouldn't make any mistake of ever thinking that we can do anything on our own.

> *"For whatever is born of God overcomes the world. And this is the victory that has overcome the world-our faith" 1 John 5:4.*

We already saw that our enemy is a spiritual being who cannot be seen with the naked eye and that our weapons are not carnal. This means that we need to operate at a level of faith to engage him. Our faith is the only weapon we have to defeat the devil.

The Apostle John explained this in his first epistle,

"For whatever is born of God overcomes the world. And this is the victory that has overcome the world-our faith" 1 John 5:4.

It is impossible to please God without faith (Hebrews 11:6), but as we exercise our faith in Him, He gives us the victory over the enemy. The victory is guaranteed as long as we abide in Christ and think not highly of ourselves more than we ought to (proverbs 3:6). Our battle is not against blood and flesh but against Satan and his troops. Remember always, no human being created in the image and likeness of God our Father can be our enemy. We must love one another as Christ loved us. If only we can learn to walk in the Spirit and not by flesh. Paul speaks of the continuous battle between the Spirit and the flesh in a letter to the church in Galatia.

"I say then: Walk in the Spirit, and you shall not fulfill the lust of the flesh. *For the* flesh *lusts against the Spirit and the Spirit against the* flesh; *and these are contrary to one another, so that you do not do the things that you wish"* Galatians 5:16-17.

I asked the Lord how does one walk in the Spirit, and His answer was that by doing what the Word of God says is walking in the Spirit. In other words, one strives to operate in the fruits of the Holy Spirit, and seeking the Spirit of Christ. Suddenly it all began to make a lot of sense to me as I found it very easy to do just that. I began to request the Holy Spirit each day to help me operate in the fruits of the Holy Spirit. I also learned to request wisdom on a daily basis just as I put on the armor of God and carry the cross daily.

These three weapons became very effective in my life and enabled me to overcome most of my personal weaknesses. I pray that you will also take this advice and request this effective armory from the Lord our God.

We know not Christ

according to the flesh

"Therefore, from now on, we regard no one according to the flesh. *Even though we have known Christ according to the* flesh, *yet now we know Him thus no longer" 2 Corinthians 5:16*

The results of a Satan dominated thoughts is considering each other as enemies. Pastor Rudzani Nemaungani once commented, *"I do not think that there is any person who wakes up in the morning and say to himself, today I am going to hurt my spouse, no one, simply because they love them"*. In the same light, I do not believe that any one can wake up and determine to hurt his brother or sister. In a letter to the church in Galatia, Paul warned them of the danger of walking in the flesh while at the same time extorting them to walk in the spirit.

"But if you bite and devour one another, beware lest you be consumed by one another! I say then: Walk in the Spirit, and you shall not fulfill the lust of the flesh. For the flesh lusts against the Spirit and the Spirit against the flesh; and these are contrary to one another, so that you do not do the things that you wish" Galatians 5:15-17.

Paul's immediate concern in this church was that they had since forgotten who their real enemy was but busy biting and devouring one another. This is a familiar site in many Christian lives today. Christians tend to lose sight of the real enemy and begin to consider each other as enemies just like this church, which to some extent leads to mistrust and hatred. This devouring and biting according to Paul, is a sign of spiritual immaturity. In a letter to the church in Corinth, he wrote,

> "And I, brethren, could not speak to you as to spiritual people but as to carnal, as to babes in Christ. I fed you with milk and not with solid food; for until now you were not able to receive it, and even now you are still not able; for you are still carnal. For where there are envy, strife, and divisions among you, are you not carnal and behaving like mere men?" 1 Corinthians 3:1-3.

The results of walking in the flesh are envy, strife which leads to biting and devouring. This kind of situation happens only when Christians don't grow spiritually, therefore giving the enemy an opportunity to influence their attitudes towards each other.

The opening passage shows us that we are not to look at man according to the flesh. This means we ought to understand that if we have not grown spiritually thereby having our lives controlled by the Holy Spirit, the course of our lives would be dictated by Satan through our flesh. We know that the flesh and the Spirit are at war with each other at any given time. If we are not at home in the Spirit therefore, we would be enslaved by the flesh. The bible says such is the intensity of the war between the Spirit and the flesh, that there is no neutrality in the life of man

(Galatians 5:16). He is influenced by either of them depending on which one has its roots deep into his personality.

Personality is a citizen of the soul and the soul is either influenced by any of the strongest between the Spirit and the flesh. It is on this basis that Paul urges us to refrain from looking at man according to the flesh but according to the Spirit. This means that we would look beyond the actions of man to find the source of influence that would then give us the correct diagnosis. What am I saying here? I am saying that because we know that the Spirit is at war with the flesh so that at any given time, man does not do what he wants to do but is influenced by either of them, we should always look beyond his actions. If at any given time we see something that seems to contradict the nature of the Spirit of truth, we know therefore that the flesh is at work.

Whenever the flesh is at play, Satan is the source of influence. Hurting each other as brethren is therefore not deliberate but an effective work of the kingdom of darkness to bring division and strife. Forgiveness therefore is a must because it is Satan who causes the tension.

Secondly, if we say we know not Christ now according to the flesh but according to the Spirit, this means we need to acknowledge that we are dead, buried and raised with Him through baptism into His death and resurrection (Romans 6:3), and as such are now seated together with Him in the heavenly place in Him (Ephesians 2:6). Simply put, the lives that we now live in the flesh, we no longer live for ourselves but for Him (Galatians 2:20). We are now complete in Christ and have the fullness of the Godhead dwelling in us in the bodily form (Colossians 2:9-10). We have become purely spiritual, no longer influenced by the flesh, and therefore apply Christ's judgment to every situation. Paul wrote in his first letter to the Corinthians,

"But he who is spiritual judges all things, yet he himself is rightly judged by no one" chapter verse 15.

Human race is under satanic attack; therefore, we should overlook their unkind deeds because they are spiritually influenced. In fact, I have realized that choosing to ignore most of the offense helps me to avoid unnecessary tensions. For example, I choose to ignore the mistakes committed by drivers on the road to avoid road rage. Thirdly, all things have spiritual connotations. The bible tells us the Old Testament was the foreshadow of the New Testament and that all seen things are made from that which is unseen, which is the Word of God.

"By faith we understand that the worlds were framed by the word of God, so that the things which are seen were not made of things which are visible" Hebrews 11:2.

This is purely spiritual transaction and the principle that governs this is applicable in our daily lives. We may not see this but our enemy who is always roaming around roaring like a lion waiting for a perfect opportunity to devour someone (1 Peter 5:8) understands this very well. He pounces on each opportunity that he can maneuver. All works of the flesh, anger, bitterness, unforgiveness, outburst of wrath etc, that are prevalent in the society and churches are conceived in the belly of hell and given birth in our churches, homes, families and society at large. But if we can understand the principle of spiritual connotation, we can never hold any grudge against any fellow human being.

Once I was watching a Nigerian film where the agents of the kingdom of darkness plotted to kill the mayor's wife. They conjured some spells and send arrows of confusion and discord in her family in order to break the marriage. The pastor of her church received a word of knowledge regarding the attack and contacted her immediately to warn her not to quarrel with any person including her husband.

Few minutes after the call, her husband came into the bedroom fuming over a tea that was given to him by the maid without sugar. He had always wanted it without sugar, but not this day. How would they have known that he wanted sugar today? But hang on; the arrows send to the house where working against him and this brought quarrel over something that did not warrant it. Fortunately, enough the wife remembered the pastor's call just in time when she wanted to answer her husband back. She quickly recognized that as a spiritual attack and asked for forgiveness for a wrong she did not commit. I must confess that I did not know this until then. I have often wondered why my wife and I would have many unnecessary quarrels over issues that really did not warrant any quarrel. What I considered a minor thing suddenly would become a huge concern to her and vice versa. I had lost sight of the spiritual warfare we Christians are involved in.

Now my prayer is that even you can understand the principle of spiritual connotation. Those where the arrows sent in the spirit to the family which manifested in the flesh and unfortunately due to lack of knowledge many marriages break because of this. Knowing our enemy and understanding his tactics would stand us in a very good position to defeat him and preserve our human relations. We would find it easy to forgive one another because we know our enemy is involved.

Anything that does not advance the kingdom of God comes from Satan. It is therefore critically imperative that we should not consider man according to the flesh but according to the Spirit at all times. Remember always, the flesh war against the Spirit and visa versa, so that man does not do what he wants to do. It is not the nature of man to be unforgiving but Satan's. By nature, man would find it easy to forgive, but if they find it difficult, it can only point to the presence of the satanic influence to the situation.

It does not matter how much convinced we are and how justifiable we may feel about the differences, the point is, we cannot withhold forgiveness against any fellow human being.

This principle became applicable in Christ's earthly ministry. God did not look at us according to the flesh but according to the Spirit. He saw what we could not see, our disparate state of affairs. Even though man rejected Him, yet because of what He knew which we were ignorant of, He soldiered on until His death on the cross. Being set free in deed is a spiritual transaction which manifests itself in the natural through our faith in Christ Jesus. So, let us therefore not consider each other according to the flesh but being spiritual by nature, we do so according to the spirit.

Man is made in the image of God

"So, God created man in His own image; in the image of God He created him; male and female He created them"
Genesis 1:27

From his album, Victims, the late Reggae music legend Lucky Dube sang a song called Different Colors/One people. Parts of the lyrics were like this, "when I see the white man, I see the image of God. When I see a black man, I see the image of God. When I see a Colored, I see the image of God. When I see a Chinese or an Indian, I see the image of God". When we were growing up in the villages, this song didn't mean anything to us. We sang along as it was a popular song then, but today having become a born-again Christian, I understand perfectly what he meant by this. Genesis 1:27 says,

"So, God created man in His own image; in the image of God He created him; male and female He created them".

The truth is none of any human being is better than any other in the eyes of God. He sees values and appreciates each one of us as His own creation. It is for this reason that even when the Christ had to come to the earth, He prepared a body for him in the likeness of man.

"Therefore, when He came into the world, He said,

„sacrifices and offering You did not desire, but a body You have prepared for Me"" Hebrews 10:5.

God created man in His image and likeness. Jesus Christ came here on earth in the likeness of man which is the likeness of God. This likeness places man at the very center of God's heart. Such an honor has been bestowed upon man only among all the created works of His hands. God has placed emphasis on man and wants man to do the same to his fellow human beings. Scriptures after scriptures emphasizes the need for all human beings to relate to one another in love and unity.

"Now I plead with you, brethren, by the name of our Lord Jesus Christ, that you all speak the same thing, and that there be no divisions among you, but that you be perfectly joined together in the same mind and in the same judgment" 1 Corinthians 1:10.

In Colossians, Paul encourages the church members to have *"their hearts knit together in love" chapter 2 verses 2.* This principle is true for all human races. Many a times as the temperature rises between people, they tend to regard one another as enemies. Instead of seeing the image of God before us, we often see an enemy that deserves to be dealt with ruthlessly, hence xenophobia and racism.

The scriptures never change though and are firm on the subject of the creation of man. God loves all of us and shows no partiality in dealing with us. Fact, man is created in the image and likeness of God. Therefore, since man is created in the image and likeness of God, whenever we see man, we see God incarnate. Under no circumstances therefore should we as people see differently from what God has ordained. We need to see the next person for what they are, a human being created in the image of God.

In other words, we should always ask ourselves this question, can I do this to God? Can I hold a grudge against my Creator? If the answer for these questions is no, (which I expect it to be) then simply put, we need to forgive the next person there and there. We cannot afford to look at man differently from how God does otherwise we are denying the truth that we are created in the image and likeness of God.

Whenever we hurt or withhold forgiveness to any human being, we are hurting and withholding forgiveness to our God and Father who continues to forgive us despite us dealing very treacherously with Him.

"Surely you did not hear, surely you did not know;surely from long ago your ear was not opened. For I knew that you would deal very treacherously, and were called a transgressor from the womb. For My name's sake I will defer My anger, and for My praise I will restrain it from you, so that I do not cut you off". Isaiah 48:8-9.

God's mercy continues to cover us even though He knew before-hand that we would deal, and not just deal but deal very treacherously with Him. But He did not hold that against us, choosing rather to defer His anger for His name's sake. Let us also defer our anger for our name's sakes.

As humans, we are created in the image of God. None of us can therefore suddenly take or manifest a different likeness or image. We would always manifest the image of God. Of course, there would be times when our accuser would seek to accuse us before our brethren, but we must always remember that we are the express image of God here on earth, radiating the brightness of His glory (Hebrews 1:3). The enemy is after this image and hates to see the position God has elevated us to in His Kingdom. It is our responsibility to guard and protect this glorious image and position by ensuring that we forgive each other there and there.

We need to always remember that Satan's hatred towards man is fueled by the fact that man was created in the very image of God. It is on this basis that James encourages the church to be careful of the tongues.

"And the tongue is fire, *a world of iniquity. The tongue is so set among our members that it defiles the whole body, and sets on* fire *the course of nature; and it set on* fire *by hell...with it we bless our God and Father, and with it we curse men, who have been made in the similitude of God"* *James 3:6;9.*

It pains me to watch in dismay as we humans continue to ravage and savage each other without a cause. I often sit and imagine this cruelty and wonder what is going on in the mind of our Father. Here are His creation, who are created with a masterpiece, busy devouring each other, for what? At the same time think how the devil sits aside and watch with pride and laughter as we children of the Most-High God continues unabated to murmur one another.

How can we become so naïve and allow ourselves to be used by the enemy who hates both of us? How can we give him so much liberty to do as he wishes with our lives? What do we gain by hating and killing each other? Even hard to swallow is when the born-again Christians speak swearing words, vulgar and corrupt words against each other in the full hearing of the holy angels. James highlighted the foolishness of this unfortunate situation:

> *"With it (the tongue) we bless our God and Father, and with it we curse men, who have been made in the similitude of God" James 3:9.*

We have the mind of Christ (1 Corinthians 2:16), the Spirit of God as well as the Spirit of Christ that makes us sons and joined heirs with Christ and makes us one with Him (Romans 8:9), let us therefore strive to please our master.

God's mercies are new every morning

"Through the Lord's mercies we are not consumed, because His compassions fail not. They are new every morning; great is Your faithfulness". Lamentations 3:22-23

I have come to the understanding that I can never fathom or measure the depth of God's mercies towards human beings. I used to meditate on the above passage, trying to figure out the mystery behind God's mercies being new every morning, until one day when the Lord brought this startling revelation to me. Some of the synonyms of the word mercy include *compassion, forgiveness, sympathy, leniency and understanding*. I found it interesting that forgiveness and understanding were among this.

As I pondered about this, I came to the understanding that the reason why God's mercies are new every morning, is that He wants to give us another chance or opportunity for a new lease of life. As the night fades away and the dawn knocks ready to usher the new day, so does his anger towards our instability and in comes the new slate from where we all need to start. The Lord does not want to hold any grudge against us hence He made the provision for forgiveness through the death of His Son, our Christ on the cross of Calvary. Jeremiah says had it not been because of His mercies, we would have been destroyed long time. But the fact that His mercies are new each morning, this gives us an opportunity to start afresh and being propelled by His compassion and leniency towards us, we strive for perfection.

As people, we should also apply the same principles to one another every day. Our Lord Jesus Christ said, *"Freely you have received and freely give" (Mathew 10:8)*. As Christians whose salvation was not an act of our own righteous works but by grace we were saved, we need to show mercy to one another.

God knew that we would deal very treacherously but yet continue to have confidence in us. We also must have confidence in our fellow human beings and show mercy, understanding, compassion and leniency to them by opening our hearts and forgiving them just as the Lord shows us mercy every morning. Let me put it this way, we were called transgressors from the womb and the fallen nature often has its way in us. Hardly the day goes by without us faltering one way or the other against our Maker.

The sins of commission and omission are reality that just won't go away from us hence we speak of God's mercy towards us the sinners. If we can understand how much we continue to sin against our Lord, yet how He has made His mercies available for us every morning, giving us an opportunity to start with a clean slate, we would find it easier to extend the same mercies to others.

It is on this basis that God says that when He forgives our sins, He does not remember them any longer (Isaiah 43:25). His new mercies wipe away all the records of the previous day and present us a clean slate from where we can commence. Can this be too hard to do? We cannot seek God's mercies unless we are prepared to show mercy to others. Our Lord Jesus said,

> *"Should you not also have had compassion on your fellow servant, just as I had pity on you?...So My Heavenly Father also will do to you if each of you, from his heart, does not forgive his brother his trespasses" Matthew 18:33,35.*

Our Lord spoke about this during His sermon on the mountain, *"Blessed are the merciful, for they shall obtain mercy" Mathew 5:7.* We cannot expect to receive the mercies of God unless we are prepared to show others the same mercy. Freely we have received mercy therefore freely we must show mercy to others. We do not have the right to withhold forgiveness towards others and expect forgiveness from Jehovah.

The measure you give, it shall be given back to you, simple as that.

God forgives for His own sake

"...But you have burdened Me with your sins; you have wearied Me with your iniquities. I, even I, am He who blots out your transgressions for My own sake; and I will not remember your sins" Isaiah 43:24-25

The phrase, *I will never forgive you*, though unfortunate, is being regularly used during many arguments. I often asked myself a question, why would the Lord choose to blot out our transgressions for His own sake not for our sake according to the passage? We are the ones who have wearied Him with our iniquities. We sin against Him, but He forgives us for His own sake not our sake yet we are the ones standing to benefit from His mercy and compassion towards us. It didn't make sense to me. I guess that is the reason I am a man and He is God in heaven above all things. But then something struck my mind just the other day.

I realized that the reason why He blots out our transgression is because He does not want to be wearied by our iniquities. You see He loves us so much to let go. Now the word wearied is synonymous to tiring, to be overloaded and weakened. God is literally saying to us, He does not want to grow weary because of our sins. He refuses to be overloaded and weakened by our many transgressions and continuous sins. Remember He knew that we would deal very treacherously with Him as we were called transgressors from the womb.

Sin is natural with man because of the transgression of Adam, one way or the other we will commit sin against Him. So instead of having to carry unnecessary loads upon His shoulders which He knows would keep on being added in anyway, He decided to do the simple, ignore and blot out. Blotting out our transgressions, for His own sake means ignoring our transgressions. This is the reason why He remembers them no longer.

How can one remember something that they never considered in the first place, you ignored it? Somebody once said, (though untested), a moment of bitterness and anger equals eight hours of human system malfunction. This means each time when we get bitter over issues and decide to vent our anger, our bodily systems are overloaded as they begin to malfunction. Anger, being an emotional state, put pressure on the heart to pump more blood to be transported throughout the body.

Unfortunately for the blood to be transported, we need more oxygen. This means the lungs have to pump at an unusual rate to be able to keep up with the rate of the heartbeat. Then, the liver must join the fray and before we know it, there is not enough oxygen, blood going through our nerves and we suffer mental breakdown in the form of nervous breakdown.

Does God need this? No, hence He decided to forgive for His

own (health) sake. Do we need this? The answer is no, we don't, hence we need to forgive for our own sake. On the other hand, it is said a moment of joy and laughter equals sixteen hours of normal system operation.

Please note that this is double the effects of anger and bitterness. No wonder it is said laughter is medicine. Ha! The bible says,

"The joy of the Lord is your strength"
(Nehemiah 8:10).

David says,

"I was glad when they said unto me come let us go to the house of the Lord, for in the presence of the Lord there is the fullness of joy (Psalms122:1)".

We know that we cannot approach God when we are bitter unless we ask Him to take away the bitterness from us, as we would not be able to hear the still, soft voice of the Holy Spirit speaking to us. Let us therefore remove all the bitterness and unforgiveness so that we can have the joy of the Lord in us which automatically strengthens us. We always remember that no matter how painful the matter maybe, we need to forgive primarily for our own sake and secondarily for the sake of our brethren. For example, it is said medically that one of the causes of ulcer is stress. Unforgiveness is the results of bitterness which unguarded causes stress.

For instance, many women who suffer from marriage related stresses do so due to bitterness and anger bottled inside over a period of time. Even a small thing would turn to be a major thing, not because it ought to be like that but rather because the outstanding issues are still weighing heavily upon their hearts. Any other small incident which might not even warrant reaction would automatically trigger the time bomb that is the results of bitterness.

Forgive others and God will forgive you

"For if you forgive men their trespasses, your heavenly Father will also forgive you. But if you do not forgive men their trespasses, neither will your Father forgive your trespasses" Mathew 6:14-15.

Christianity as a religion is based on forgiveness. Forgiveness is at the very core of the message of salvation. Even though we have not known or seen Christ with our own eyes, yet we believe that through His death we have redemption and forgiveness of our sins. Basically, what this means is that our Father has made provision for the forgiveness of our sins, whenever we approach Him with repentant hearts.

In a nutshell, we can safely say, God is more than willing to forgive us. But His willingness to forgive us is dependent upon us acknowledging that we are sinners and asking forgiveness. Let us firstly see how the prophet Jeremiah addresses this issue:

"Only acknowledge your iniquity, that you have transgressed against the Lord your God" chapter 3 verse 13.

Our Father is willing to forgive us provided we take full responsibilities by acknowledging our sinfulness. Furthermore, we need to understand that just as we are subjected to mistakes and faults, so does the rest of humanity. Whenever we transgress, we ask for forgiveness and expect God to forgive us as He promised to according to Scripture.

"If we say that we have no sin, we deceive ourselves, and the truth is not in us. If we confess our sins, He is faithful and just to forgive us our sins and cleansesu from all unrighteousness". 1 John 1:8-9

We must always take into consideration that we ourselves were forgiven by our Father in that while we were still sinners Christ died for us on the cross. This means that even though we were immersed in sinfulness, our Father chose to ignore our iniquities by justifying us.

"Moreover, whom He predestined, these He also called; whom He called, these He also justified; and whom He justified, these He also glorified" Romans 8:30.

God did not forgive us because we deserved it, but He forgave us on His own accord. It was His choice to forgive us. We must therefore apply the same principle to each other. The all-knowing God decided to wipe away our sins and give us a clean slate through His Son Jesus Christ. Isaiah has this to say:

"Surely you did not hear, surely you did not know; surely from long ago your ear was not opened. For I knew that

you would deal very treacherously, and were called a transgressor from the womb. For My name's sake I will defer My anger, and for My praise I will restrain it from you, so that I do not cut you off". Isaiah 48:8-9.

Long before we came into the picture, God knew us. David added,

"Your eyes saw my substance, being yet unformed. And in Your book, they were all written, the days fashioned for me, when as yet there were none of them" Psalm 139:16.

In Jeremiah, God shares with us His inside knowledge into man,

"Before I formed you in the womb, I knew you; before you were born, I sanctified you; I ordained you a prophet to the nations" Jeremiah 1:5.

"Surely you did not hear, surely you did not know; surely from long ago your ear was not opened. For I knew that you would deal very treacherously, and were called a transgressor from the womb. For My name's sake I will defer My anger, and for My praise I will restrain it from you, so that I do not cut you off", Isaiah 48:8-9.

Scripture after scripture, we can clearly see God's in-depth knowledge of man. The bible tells us that Jesus was preordained for the purpose of our Salvation before the foundation of the earth.

> *"He indeed was foreordained before the foundation of the world, but was manifest in these last times for you" 1 Peter 1:20.*

God, who declares the end from the beginning, knew that we would deal treacherously with Him and made provision for the forgiveness of our sins through the cross. He did not expect us to be perfect at all times. He knew that we would falter and make mistakes. Basically, what this means is that, God saw our wrong ways before the foundation of the earth, yet even that did not stop Him from justifying us. The word, justify means having a soft spot for somebody. Even though the person is wrong, you choose to ignore or rub off the mistakes, choosing rather to look at their good works.

God justified us not because we were righteous but because He decided to do it anyway. Human beings are subjected to mistakes. As God chose to ignore our wrongs so we should we choose forgiveness under any circumstances.

> *"And whenever you stand praying, if you have anything against anyone, forgive him that your Father in heaven may also forgive you your trespasses. But if you do not forgive, either will your Father in heaven forgive your trespasses" Mark 11:25-26.*

Now that we know the truth of our Father's forgiveness of our own sins, we should also apply the same principle of forgiveness which He used to us to others as well. When dealing with forgiveness, one should always remember the parable of a servant whom the king forgave his debts, only for him to go and throw his own brother who owed him into prison. He owed the king more than what his brother owed him and though his king forgave him and cancelled his debts, he however chose to deal harshly with his brother (Matthew 18:23-35). This parable teaches us that we should under no circumstance refuse to forgive one another because our Father forgave us worse sins than our brethren have committed against us.

Let us put this parable in monetary value. This wicked servant owed the king ten thousand talents. Let's say one talent equals one rand. This means the servant owed the king ten thousand rand. He could not pay the debt and the king according to the standard of the day, wanted to sell him, his wife and children and all that he had to recover the money. But the servant pleaded with him to be patient with him as he needed some time to repay the total amount. But upon hearing his pleading, the king had compassion on him and forgave/cancelled the debt. The king did not give him a chance to repay his debt but cancelled the debt.

But this same servant went out and found his brother who owed him hundred denarii which was much less than what he owed the king. An equivalent of hundred rand as compared to the ten thousand he was forgiven. Instead of showing the same mercy to his brother as was showed to him by the king, the bible says he laid hands on him, taking him by the throat saying pay me what you owe me. Although his brother pleaded with him in the same manner he did with the king, he however took his brother and threw him into the prison until he should pay the debt. He was forgiven ten thousand rand but refused to forgive hundred denarii let alone give his brother a chance to pay the hundred rand owed to him. Upon hearing this, the king was furious with him.

> *"So, when his fellow servants saw what had been done, they were very grieved, and came and told their master all that had been done. Then his master, after he had called him, said to him, „You wicked servant! I forgave you all the debt because you begged me. Should you not also have had compassion on your fellow servant, just as I had pity on you?" And his master was angry, and delivered him to the torturers until he should pay all that was due to him. So, My heavenly Father also will do to you if each of you, from his heart, does not forgive his brother his trespasses"* (Mathew 18:31-35).

Many of us don't realize how much in trouble we are with God. On numerous occasions our Lord Jesus kept on reminding us about the worms that never dies and fires that are never quenched in hell. There is a song that says I will never know how much it costs to see my sins upon the cross, and surely my brethren, we will never know how much it costs our Lord Jesus to purchase us from the devil.

"For you were bought at a price"1 Corinthians 6:20.

The truth is we were in big trouble until the cross. Through His Son, our Father forgave us all our trespasses and washed us clean. We can never do enough to repay the kindness no matter how many years we live here on earth. We deserved death, but His grace became sufficient for us. He chose to forgive us and so should we forgive those who trespassed against us. If we consider what God has done for us, it should be easy for us to forgive others just as our Father forgave us. Surely if we say we deserve to be forgiven by our Father, other people also deserve to be forgiven by us. If we refuse to forgive, we should also know that our Father will not forgive us. Christ made it clear when teaching the disciples how to pray.

"And forgive us our debts, as we forgive our debtors"
Matthew 6:12.

Now the word, as in this sentence implies that our being forgiven by our Father is directly dependent upon us forgiving our debtors/others. If we forgive others, He will forgive us but if we don't forgive them, He also won't forgive us our own trespasses.

"So, My heavenly Father also will do to you if each of you,
from his heart, does not forgive his brother his trespasses"
Matthew 18:35.

Therefore, for our own sake, let us refrain from holding grudges against one another but rather let us strive to live at peace with each other more so that we are married to the same King and have become one with Him.

Love your neighbor as you love yourself

"And the second, like it, is this: „You shall love your neighbor as yourself" Mark 12:31

The Scribes have come to Jesus seeking to trap Him by asking which one among the Ten Commandments was the first. His answer was straight forward and two-fold. He gave them the first commandment as,

"And you shall love the Lord your God with all your heart, with all your soul, with all your mind, and with all your strength" Mark 12:30.

After addressing God as the first love, Jesus gave them the second most important commandment.

"You shall love your neighbor as yourself" Mark 12:31.

It is important to note that any person other than yourself is regarded as your neighbor. In other words, my spouse is my neighbor in the same way that my son is. As long as it is not me, then whoever the next person is, is my neighbor! Now the bible says we must love our neighbors as we love ourselves. Paul took this commandment further when he addressed conduct of husbands towards their wives,

"So, husbands ought to love their own wives as their own bodies; he who loves his wife loves himself. For no one ever hated his own flesh, but nourishes and cherishes it, just as the Lord does the church" Ephesians 5:28-29.

Whenever the word so, is used at the beginning of a sentence, we need to look at the preceding sentence to get the whole meaning. In this case Paul explains to us how Christ loved the church and gave His life for her, to present her blameless, not having a spot, wrinkle or any such thing (verse 27).

The word, 'so' was used in the context that as Christ loved the church and gave Himself for her, so should husbands love their wives to the extent of giving their lives for them. Paul acknowledges here that the wife becomes the husband's neighbor whom he must love the same way he loves himself.

In other words, man ought to love his neighbor as he loves (the same way, with same passion and tender) himself. The result of this kind of love is that man would never hurt another man as,

"No one ever hated his own flesh, *but nourished*

and cherished it, even as the Lord the church"

Ephesians5:29

This means if this principle is applied, we would never have a situation where people hated each other as the bible is clear regarding hating oneself. The only time man would ever hate his own flesh is when we have demonic influence. Human beings are communal beings, called to share and live among others. Therefore, it is of utmost importance, that we understand the neighbor-neighbor relations. As neighbors, we forgive unconditionally. When I make a mistake which affects my life, I don't get angry and start punishing myself, cutting myself into pieces.

I can be angry with myself for some few minutes but that is just it. The same process should apply with our neighbors. This is why the bible says, *"Be angry but do not sin. Don't let the sun go down in your wrath. Neither give place to the devil" Ephesians 4:26-27.* We are allowed to be angry for a moment but our anger should never lead us to sin as this would open us up for attacks by Satan. Active sin in our lives gives him the legal ground. For the umpteenth time, we can see that there is no room for unforgiveness.

Seventy Times Seven Principles

"Jesus said to him, „I do not say to you, up to seven times, but up to seventy times seven" Matthew 18:22

The above was the Christ's response to Peter's question regarding the number of times he needed to forgive his brother who keeps on sinning against him. My understanding of Jesus response is that there is no room for unforgiveness. I calculated seventy times seven and came to a figure of four hundred and ninety. This means my neighbor has to offend me four hundred and ninety times in a day before I can say it is enough. How did I come to a time frame whereas Jesus did not give one? Well, simply because the bible tells us that we should not let the sun set in our anger. With this command in mind, I then used this to presume that when Jesus spoke about the seventy times seven, He meant to use it in a day.

This means I can only count that particular day as long as it has not yet set. Knowing also therefore that the Lord's mercies are new every day, the seventy times seven becomes applicable each day. I came to understand this when the Lord explained how His mercies work. You see, each day the Lord starts us with a clean slate as His mercies are new every day. This is because His unconditional love towards us covers the multitudes of our sins.

"Hatred stirs up strife, but love covers all sins" Proverbs 10:12.

Our Father therefore expects us to use the same principle in showing mercy towards others. We have freely received His mercies and we in turn should freely show mercies towards others in the same way God shows us His mercies.

"Blessed are the merciful, for they shall obtain mercy" Mathew 5:7.

We also are not perfect and therefore should understand that others are in the same way not perfect as well. To be honest, it is literally impossible for any man to sin against another man seventy times seven in a single day. What is our Lord Jesus therefore saying to us? That it is a spiritual crime for any man not to forgive another man. There is absolutely no room for unforgiveness for those who are blood washed by the precious blood of Jesus Christ. Once again, I quote the words of Dr. Charles Stanley, *"we don't have a right to withhold forgiveness from anyone, and that certainly includes our friends"*.

Our God set precedence for us

"Then Jesus said, „Father, forgive them, for they do not know what they do"" Luke 23:34

It is very sad to hear and see many of our people blaming others when they themselves have so many skeletons in their cupboard. Our Lord Jesus Christ admonished us to look within ourselves first before we can begin to accuse our brothers.

"And why do you look at the speck in your brother's eye, but do not consider the plank in your own eye? Or how can you say to your brother, „let me remove the speck from your eye", and look, a plank is in your own eye? Hypocrite! First remove the plank from your own eye, and then you will see clearly to remove the speck from your brother's eye" Mathew 7:3-5.

Many of us violate the above scripture on daily basis. We are often too quick to look at other's faults while we ignore our very own. The truth is no man is righteous. Each day is lived by God's grace. It is on this basis that we need to strive to imitate Him at all costs. Our own God who has made the heaven His throne and the earth His foot stool, the Creator of the heavens and the earth, the Master of all things; chose to manifest in the form of man and be humiliated in all possible way that man could ever be for our sake. The book of Hebrews records it this way,

"Sacrifice and offering You did not desire, but a body You have prepared for Me. In burnt offerings and sacrifices for sin You had no pleasure. Then I said, „Behold, I have come-in the volume of the book it is written of Me-to do Your will, O God" chapter 10:5-7 (quoted from the book of Psalms 40:6-8).

And Paul in his first letter to Timothy, he put it in this manner:

"And without controversy great is the mystery of godliness: God was manifested in the flesh, *justified in the Spirit, seen by angels, preached among the Gentiles, believed on in the world, received up in glory" 1 Timothy 3:16.*

Our Father could have used a different way to redeem mankind. All things are possible with God yet He chose this path which would see Him at the mercy of His creation, mankind. Christ who in His nature is God surrendered Himself to the hands of man.

"He was oppressed and He was afflicted, yet He opened not His mouth; He was led as a lamb to the slaughter, and as a sheep before its shearers is silent, so He opened not His mouth" Isaiah 53:7

Did He have no power as the soldiers scorning Him suggested? Of course not! Christ had earlier told Peter that He could have easily commanded the twelve legions of angels to deal with the soldiers but chose not to. He had to humble Himself and give His life over to the cross. The cross was said to be the most humiliating form of death as it carries with it the curse.

"His body shall not remain overnight on the tree, but you shall surely bury him that day, so that you do not defile the land which the Lord your God is giving you as an inheritance; for he who is hanged is accursed of God" *Deuteronomy 21:23*

Although Jesus had power and authority, He chose to waiver them, the ability which we as humans continue to abuse quite often. Although He committed neither crime nor any treason worthy of death, He humbled Himself before them and have them hang Him this was because Christ knew better than what they knew.

"For My thoughts are not your thoughts, nor are your ways My ways", says the Lord. "For as the heavens are higher than the earth, so are My ways higher than your ways, and My thoughts than your thoughts" Isaiah 55:8-9.

It is therefore important even in our lives that we disregard the quarrels because of what we know that our neighbors don't know. This does not make us foolish, but rather put us in a position to convince our neighbors of God's undying love.

"Let this mind be in you which was also in Christ Jesus" *Philippians 2:4*

You see our Father knew that there is value in each one of us hence He was willing through His Son to be humiliated for our sake. Without that sacrifice, we could never have had any chance of eternity with Him. The same principle should be applicable in our daily interactive with our neighbors. We must never devalue any human being but always consider the value each human being has. Our knowledge and understanding of the value of each human being should put us in a pole position to be willing to be humiliated for the sake of others.

For this reason, we must approach the throne of grace daily and ask the grace of yielding. This grace will enable us to be at peace even when we are humiliated. They say that humility can never be humiliated. Simply put, due to the immerse knowledge we have of the value each human being has, we would always be willing to accept their wrongs and forgive without any hassles. This is the attitude our Lord demonstrated while here on earth and as Paul said, we must strive to embrace this attitude every day of our lives.

There are many other cases that we can refer to within the scriptures of heroes of faith who cried forgive them for they know not what they do. Stephen's story in the book of Acts comes to mind immediately. An Israelite by birth, he preached the message of the cross to the multitudes and they rejected the truth and chose rather to stone him to death. It was on this instance that facing death and seeing the Son the Man standing at the right side of the Father's throne, that he cried forgive them for they know not what they do.

> *"When they heard these things, they were cut to the heart, and they gnashed at him with their teeth. But he, being full of the Holy Spirit, gazed into heaven and saw the glory of God, and Jesus standing at the right hand of God, and said, „Look! I see the heavens opened and the Son of Man standing at the right hand of God!" Then they cried out with a loud voice, stopped their ears, and ran at him with one accord; and they cast him out of the city and stoned him. And the witnesses laid down their clothes at the feet of a young man names Saul. And they stoned Stephen as he was calling on God and saying, „Lord Jesus, receive my spirit". Then he knelt down and cried out with a loud voice, „Lord, do not charge them with this sin". And when he had said this, he fell asleep" Acts 7:54-60.*

How many of us can say such words when we are being hurt? The right thing would be to cry justice and revenge but that is not the nature of God. His nature is of love and forgiveness. Stephen understood that they didn't have the knowledge as well as being baptized with the Holy Spirit as he was. Their ignorance was thus justifiable. As such could not see what he saw when the heavens opened up before his eyes as vindication to his preaching and what was about to happen as a result of people's reaction to the sermon. Stephen chose to forgive when he had the choice of being bitter.

Paul also chose to forgive when harm was done to him. He felt betrayed by his comrades/brethren when he was left alone to defend the gospel after his fellow Christians deserted him in the hour of need. But likewise, he chose to forgive and pleaded with God not to charge them either.

> *"At my first defenses no one stood with me, but all forsook me. May it not be charged against them"* 2 Timothy 4:16

It important therefore that we also learn from these heroes of faith and follow in their footstep, always remembering that what happened to them became our examples and were written for our own admonition.

> *"Now all these things happened to them as examples, and they were written for our admonition, upon whom the ends of the ages have come"* 1 Corinthians 10:11.

Let us seek therefore forgiveness and learn to forgive those who have trespassed against us. There should remain in our lives no longer any room for unforgiveness as the night is almost spent and the day at hand. Our Lord Jesus is coming soon.

Part Two

The Devastating

Consequences of

Unforgiveness

The harsh reality of unforgiveness

"Be sober, be vigilante; because your adversary the devil walks about like a roaring lion, seeking whom he may devour" 1 Peter 5:8

Now having dealt with few deliverance cases both within and outside the church, I have come upon some very disturbing realities of the burden of unforgiveness during the sessions. We have been praying for Johanna (not the real name) for some time now without success. The demons would leave but would soon be back again tormenting the sister. This particular spirit had caused her to fall asleep at work while she was still on three months' probation at her new job. They had found her asleep on her desk and refused to give her employment due to that.

During the deliverance session, I could see the spirits wanted to leave but they somehow seemed to be blocked by something else. It had been two hours of prayer and I was beginning to be tired and already contemplating stopping the session. Demons kept on manifesting pride, refusing to leave the sister. As we asked them later what hindered them from coming out, they said they were being blocked by unforgiveness as the sister refuses to forgive people who have hurt her in the past and have thus opened the door into her life.

This door was therefore being manned by the spirit of

unforgiveness who had become the gatekeeper, allowing and refusing access and exit to many other demons. As they were now feeling the heat of the power of God, they wanted to leave but were blocked by the gatekeeper as he was not addressed by name.

They continued to elaborate how she had refused to forgive people who had hurt her and through that opened door, they had found their way in her life. Any deliverance attempts without firstly dealing with this particular unforgivess spirit would yield no return, and this opened door would cause more woes to follow her until she closes it completely by voluntarily forgiving any person who had hurt her.

We commanded the demons to withdraw so that we could speak to her. Johanna explained to us her story and we requested her to forgive anyone who had hurt. It was only after she confessed and forgiven them that the spirits left without any further hassle. From that day, I learnt how dangerous unforgiveness is and what dangers it can lead a person to. The bible says,

> "Blessed are the pure in heart for they shall see God"
> Mathew 6:8.

I am sure each one of us can't wait to see God and experience His powerful presence in our lives. But as long as one is bitter, he cannot see God, as out of the abundance of his heart, his mouth will speak bitter swelling words. God wants a pure heart, but there is no purity where bitterness and unforgiveness reside. In fact, any active sin in our lives will render our communication with our Creator ineffective.

Demons ultimate purpose is to block the believer from experiencing God in their lives thereby rendering them fruitless in the days of their lives here on earth. This will improve the chances of us being thrown out of heaven and be cast into outer darkness as the unprofitable servants.

> *"And cast the unprofitable servant into the outer darkness, There, will be weeping and gnashing of teeth" Mathew 25:30*

They know that this would not please our Father who wants each one of us to bear fruits of endurance (John 15:5). Our Lord Jesus said in Mathew chapter eleven:

> *"Come to Me, all you who labor and are heavy laden, and I will give you rest. Take My yoke upon you and learn from Me, for I am gentle and lowly in heart, and you will find rest for your souls. For my yoke is easy and My burden is light" verses 28-30.*

The Lord Jesus is giving us the way out of our current burdens of unforgiveness, would you my brother/sister, mother, father bring your heavy loads to His shoulders. He wants to carry them for you. He can see that they are too heavy for you and want to rescue you. On numerous occasions, God has urged us to cast all our care upon Him (1 Peter 5:7). In a letter to the church in Phillip, Paul urged them *to,*

"Be anxious for nothing, but in everything by prayer and supplication, with thanksgiving, let your requests be made known to God" (chapter 4:6).

This he said would enable, *"the peace of God, which surpasses all understanding, to guard your hearts and minds through Christ Jesus" (verse 7).*

Unforgiveness is a very bitter pill to swallow. It is like cancer that spreads throughout the entire body until it has finally absorbed itself into every system of your body. Unless it is burnt out while still in the early stages, it has the potential to cause major damage even to a point of death to a person, so does unforgiveness. Therefore, my brother, take my advice and avoid it at all costs. Consider what the writer of the book of Hebrews says,

"You have not yet resisted to bloodshed, striving against sin" Hebrews 12:4.

It is our responsibility to resist un-forgiveness and strive against it even unto bloodshed. We should never allow this cancer to spread throughout our bodies. Never!

Unforgiveness separates us from God

"Behold, the Lord's hand is not shortened, that it cannot save; nor His ear heavy, that it cannot hear. But your iniquities have separated you from your God; and your sins have hidden His face from you, so that He will not hear" Isaiah 59:1-2

The problem with sin is that it separates us from our Father. We need to remember always that unforgiveness is sin and it is a direct disobedience to God's command to forgive one another as He has forgiven us. Every sin is our lives give our enemy Satan legal right over our lives.

"He who digs a pit will fall into it. And whoever breaks through a wall will be bitten by a serpent" Ecclesiastes 10:8.

The other version put it this way…*he who breaks the hedge, the serpent shall bite him.* God promised to be a wall of fire round about His children and hedge us in front and behind (Zechariah 2:5). This is maximum protection and nothing shall by any means touch them. But any active sin in our lives automatically breaks the very hedge God had made around us, and the bible promises us that, he who breaks the hedge the serpent shall definitely bite him (Ecclesiastes 10:8). This means our enemy would pounce on this and hit us hard by cutting the communication and relations we have with God. It is on this basis that God urges us,

"Only acknowledge your iniquity, that you have transgressed against the Lord your God..." Jeremiah 3:13.

Unforgiveness is an abomination before God. He hates it with a passion. Anyone found withholding forgiveness to his brother would receive no forgiveness from God. The passage we read in Isaiah 59 tells us that our iniquities separate us from God. He who is separated from God has no chance against Satan.

We have already read the story of a sister who was delivered in the church. A close analysis of her situation brings one to this conclusion. Any active sin in our lives will separate us from God and this has always been the plan of the devil. It is therefore our responsibilities to seek to draw closer to God.

"Therefore, submit to God. Resist the devil and he will flee from you. Draw near to God and He will draw near to you" James 4:7-8.

If you are reading this book and have a bitter heart over some incident/s that happened in the past, I urge you my friend to release the hurt from your heart less the enemy should pounce on that and block you from experiencing the fellowship with God our Father.

Simply put, unforgiveness is demonic and anything demonic is a deadly poison to humanity. Jesus Christ died to set us free from such demonic powers and we would do well to accept the free gift our Father gave us. Father has reconciled us back to Himself through Christ and He desires that we should have fellowship with Him until eternity (2 Corinthians 5:18). These works have been finished from the foundation of the world, but the onus is on us to accept the free gift and seek fellowship with Him by obeying His commands to forgive one another even as He has unconditionally forgiven us (Hebrews 4:3). It is on this basis that He said through Peter,

"Therefore, brethren, be even more diligent to make your call and election sure, for if you do these things, you will never stumble; for so an entrance will be supplied to you abundantly into the everlasting kingdom of our Lord and Savior Jesus Christ" 2 Peter 1:10-11.

Any active sin in our lives will keep us from God. In a prayer of repentance, David cried out unto the Lord after his unfortunate incident with Bathsheba, the wife of Uriah the Hittite.

"When I kept silent, my bones grew old through my groaning all the day long. For day and night Your hand was heavy upon me; my vitality was turned into the drought of summer" Psalm 32:3-4.

David acknowledges that his active unconfessed sin shut all the doors of contact with God in his life. As a result of this wall which now exists between him and God, his vitality had turned into the drought of summer. He realizes here that he was now far from God hence his further pleading with God after confessing his sin,

"Make me hear joy and gladness, that the bones You have broken may rejoice. Hide Your face from my sins, and blot out all my iniquities. Create in me a clean heart, O God, and renew a steadfast spirit within me. Do not cast me away from Your presence, and do not take Your Holy Spirit from me. Restore to me the joy of salvation, and uphold me by Your generous Spirit". Psalms 51:8-12.

Let us look at few things here and learn. First, we need to remember that unforgiveness is sin which is treated like any other sin by God who views all sins as abomination. The presence of sin in our lives robs us of the joy of the Lord which is our strength. As long as we are far from Him, we can never experience His joy, for it is written,

"In the presence of the Lord, there is the fullness of joy" (Psalm 16:11).

This means, in the absence of the Lord, there is misery. We don't need that, do we? Secondly, since „the joy of the Lord is our strength (Nehemiah 8:10,), with his relationship with God having become sour, David says his vitality had turned into the drought of summer. He had neither life nor strength to go on. Paul says,

"I can do all things through Christ who strengthens me" (Philippians 4:13).

Without God, we can accomplish nothing, absolutely nothing.

Thirdly, David talks about the lack of excitement in his salvation. The truth is there is excitement in being a born-again Christian. But sin suffocates this excitement and what is left is life of misery, hence the cry, saying, *"Restore to me the joy of salvation, and uphold me by Your generous Spirit"*. Without the Lord and the hope of salvation, there is nothing in life to be excited about. It is on this basis that you see people committing suicide. They have no hope because they don't have the Christ who is the hope of our glory in them. We should not suffocate ourselves and render our spirits retarded by harboring bitterness and unforgiveness.

Such acts are unnecessary and seek only to bring us into bondage. Lastly, David requests God to *"Create in me a clean heart, O God, and renew a steadfast spirit within me"*. I reckon that this is the prayer that we should each make. The amount of bitterness cannot be just removed without our Father's intervention. We need Him to renew a steadfast spirit within us if we have any ambition of making it in life eternally with Him by His side in the city of gold, the New Jerusalem. Our sufficiency cometh from Him for He knows the thoughts that He has for us, the thoughts of peace not of evil, to give us a future and a hope (Jeremiah 29:11).

Unforgiveness enslaves

"Come to Me, all you who labor and are heavy laden, and I will give you rest. Take My yoke upon you and learn from Me, for I am gentle and lowly in heart, and you will find rest for your souls. For My yoke is easy and My burden is light" Mathew 11:28-30

Once a certain Evangelist gave an illustration of how burdened people behave during his meeting. He said there was once an old woman who was walking along the road, carrying her child at the back with a bag on her head. A man who was traveling along the same route stopped and gave her a lift. She gladly accepted the offer and jumped at the back of the van. As the man was driving, he noticed something strange through the back window. The woman he had given lift to with the intention of resting her from what seems to be a heavy burden of a child and a bag and a long journey, was sitting at the back still carrying the bag on her head and the baby on her back. She didn't put any down to rest.

In the same, even after the Son of man had come and liberated us from the burden of sin, many of our people still continue to carry those sins along the path of salvation. The bible records that; if the Son sets you free, you are free indeed (John 8:36). Christ has redeemed us from the curse of the law having become a curse for us (Galatians 3:13), and it is now up to us to ensure that we maintain our liberty.

"Stand fast therefore in the liberty by which Christ has made us free, and do not be entangled again with a yoke of bondage" Galatians 5:1.

Why should we allow unforgiveness to bring us into bondage again when Christ had set us free? **UNFORGIVENESS ENSLAVES HIM WHO ENTERTAINS IT**. It grabs its victim and holds him tight until he suffocates. Peter warns, *"...for by whom a person is overcome, by him also he is brought into bondage" 2 Peter 2:19.*

In most cases the person to whom we hold grudges against, have no idea how we are feeling about them. They go on in life without any problem while we have to take the pain of the cancer spreading within our systems. We have problem with people who have no problem with us. This is vanity and striving against the wind. We are fighting a losing battle. It is rather important that we should take heed to what Paul says in his letter to the Galatians.

"For you, brethren, have been called to liberty; only do not use liberty as an opportunity for the flesh, but through love serve one another" Chapter 5:13.

His advice to us is to refrain from giving the flesh an opportunity to enslave us. In the same letter, Paul gives us an idea of what the fruits of the flesh are. Among others he mentions envy, jealousy, hatred and sorcery which are nothing but jealousy and envy manipulated by demons. All the cases of sorcery or witchcraft emanated from jealousy and envy. A person becomes bitter because someone is prospering. Yes, people will prosper if they don't have bitterness and unforgiveness. Once a person allows jealousy and envy to take root in their lives, the next stop is witchcraft. Our Lord Jesus said,

"You have heard that it was said to those of old,

„You shall not murder" and whoever murders will be in danger of the judgment". But I say to you that whoever is angry with his brother without a cause shall be in danger of the judgment"" Mathew 5:21-23.

Because they have broken the hedge, the serpent finds it easier to bite them. The unprotected ground of their lives becomes the demonic play-ground. It is here where the demons of witchcraft will fuel the hatred to a point of murder. Once you reach this point, there is no turning back.

Having said that, this is not the only thing demons can do to an unprotected ground. Many other things can be introduced i.e. sexual immorality and the like. The purpose here is to have total control over your soul influencing your emotions, your will and your intellectual abilities. The enemy is able to manipulate such a person to an extent of total mental incapacity. This is not what Christ died for my brethren. It is completely opposite the freedom that He promised us. The story of King David's son Absalom shed some serious light into the demonic activities through unforgiveness. The story is found in the book of second Samuel chapter 13.

Amnon, his half-brother had raped his sister Tamar after he pretended to be ill and requesting his father David to send Tamar to cook for him after the king had checked on him. After hearing this, the bible records that Absalom spoke to his brother Amnon neither good nor bad. It was only after two full years when everyone had forgotten about the unfortunate incident that Absalom killed his brother, Amnon. This is how the bible puts the words of Jonadad the son of Shimeah, David's brother when he reported to David the incident,

"For by the command of Absalom this has been determined from the day that he forced his sister Tamar", verse 32.

Please note that for full two years, Absalom lived with bitterness within his heart until the Devil manipulated this bitterness to commit murder. As a result of unforgiveness, Absalom became a murderer who went on to force a coup de tat in his father's kingdom. After his father, King David fled the city of Jerusalem, Absalom did one of the wicked things ever done in Israel, and he went in on all his father's concubines. His life became controversial until his death at the hand of Joab, king David's lieutenant. He could have avoided all this though, had he forgiven his brother Amnon for the dreadful thing he did to his sister Tamar.

Both Christ and Stephen had opportunity to be bitter after what happened to them. But in both cases, they choose to extent an olive branch towards their enemies, pleading for unconditional pardon from God the Father on their behalf. Jesus on the cross after being beaten thirty-nine times then crucified. Jesus said,

> "Father, forgive them, for they do not know what they do." (Luke 23:34).

And they divided His garments and casts lots. Then we see Stephen being stoned for preaching the gospel of salvation to his own people.

> "Then he knelt down and cried out with a loud voice, „Lord, do not charge them with this sin‟" (Acts 7:60).

Both these men felt justified to demand retribution, but instead of demanding it, rather they chose the path of unconditional forgiveness. This is a lesson to us all, that no matter how strong we might feel we have a case against our brethren, we have a duty to forgive each other unconditionally.

Part Three

Practical Steps To Remove Huddles Of Unforgiveness

The road ahead

We need to remember that people who are bitter and thus unforgiving are no longer themselves. They are trapped and unable to help themselves. They cannot release themselves from the trap and hole they have fallen in and need someone from the outside to assist by pulling them. Below we shall discuss several means and ways provided by the scriptures on how we can best help address and alleviate the problem. Huddles need to be removed and crooked path straightened up. It is not going to be easy because the road is rough and needs to be smoothened.

The Lord promised Cyrus that He will go before him to do among other things, straighten the path, smoothen the road, smash down the gates of iron and break in pieces the gates of brass while opening for him double doors.

> "Thus, says the Lord to His anointed, to Cyrus, whose **right hand I have held**, to subdue nations before him and loose the armor of kings, to open before him the double doors so that the gates will not be shut. I will go before you, and make the crooked places straight; I will break in pieces the gates of bronze, and cut the gates of iron" Isaiah 45:1-2.

The Lord is holding the hand of His anointed. We also need to hold the hand of our spouse/relation.

They cannot do this alone. The enemy has raised and fortified the defenses with gates of iron and brass. It is an impenetrable fortress. No man can conquer while fighting alone. Let us help smoothen the rough roads and straighten the crooked path and be patient with them.

Deal with forgiveness the Godly way

"Moreover, if your brother sins against you, go and tell him his fault between you and him alone. If he hears you, you have gained your brother. But if he will not hear, take with you one or two more, that „by the mouth of two or three witnesses every word may be established". And if he refuses to hear them, tell it to the church. But if he refuses even to hear the church, let him be to you like a heathen and a tax collector" Matthew18:15-17

Only if we can understand God's working principles. Many of us have by-passed the above principle many times when we are faced with a challenge of unforgiveness. The bible gives us three things used as protocol in dealing with differences. Firstly, Jesus mentions that, *"If your brother sins against you, go and tell him his fault between you and him alone".* The responsibility here is given to the one who has been wronged.

In other words, if I am the complainant, I must take the first step and approach my spouse to make her aware of the offence she committed against me. Sometimes she may not even be aware that she has offended me, therefore it is my duty to let her know. There are many cases today of people being bitter towards others who are not even aware they have offended them. This can be avoided by letting the person know how you feel.

The second important thing that Jesus mentions here is that

I should go to my brother and speak   to him between us. In other words, this is a matter between two individuals only. The attitude that I the complainant should have, should always be to gain my brother. We should always remember that we have a duty as Christians towards each other. I shouldn't go to him with the intention of crucifying him but rather to show him his fault and gain him.

Couples have a duty towards each other not only as couples but as Christians as well. We must always remember that we have responsibility towards each other, firstly as Christian brothers and sisters and secondly as husbands and wives. We need to help each other enter the narrow gate. Heaven is beckoning for both of us and therefore our duty towards each other cannot be over emphasized enough. One member cannot enter heaven while the other goes to hell.

> "Therefore, a man shall leave his father and mother and be joined to his wife, and they shall become one flesh" Genesis 2:24.

So, we no longer talk about two but one. It is therefore imperative that both assist each other to enter the narrow gate for two is better than one, for when one falls the other picks him up and vice versa. Peter put this more clearly in his first letter to the church addressing marriage issues in relations to serving and suffering for God's glory:

"Wives, likewise, be submissive to your own husbands, that even if some do not obey the word, they, without a word, may be won by the conduct of their wives. For in this manner, in former times, the holy women who trusted in God also adorned themselves, being submissive to their own husbands. Husbands, likewise, dwell with them with understanding, giving honor to the wife, as to the weaker vessel, and as being heirs together of the grace of life, that your prayers may not be hindered. Finally, all of you be of one mind, having compassion for one another, love as brothers, be tenderhearted, be courteous; not returning evil for evil or reviling for reviling, but on the contrary blessing, knowing that you were called to this, that you may inherit a blessing" 1 Peter 3:1, 5, 7-9.

The problem that we have is that most cases, couples approach each other with the intention of winning the argument or proving the other wrong.

This approach does not work because it advances selfishness, in that it says I am right and you are wrong. Unfortunately, this very approach has spilled into the church and many brethren are also falling into the trap of selfishness and self-centeredness.

But if the brother will not hear, we are instructed to take one or two more along for further engagements. Again, here the purpose should not be to proof our spouse or brother wrong but to seek amicable solution to the impasse. I have personally struggled with this. As the Lord brought this principle to my attention,

I found it difficult to practice it in my own life. In most cases when I had differences with my wife, I would seek to speak to the friend that I know would always sympathize with me.

Our discussion never had any intention of winning back my wife but always to proof how bad she was. Not even a single day have I requested him to mediate between us as the scriptures require. This is not right as the objective should always be to gain my spouse. In the above passage, Peter reminds us of our responsibilities towards one another. We are always to remember that we are heirs together of the grace of life and that we must be of one mind, having compassion for one another and above all love as brothers.

Firstly, I cannot share this with any man before I bring it to my wife's attention that she has wronged me. Secondly, whenever I decide to involve the second or the third person, this should always be with the intention of getting them to mediate between us. The next step to take would be to inform the church, if he refuses to hear the other two people. By this time the matter should be resolved. In a letter to the church in Corinth, Paul urged them not to take each other to court before the heathen. He advocated the use of the church channels in dispute resolutions rather than taking each other before the court where the matter would be presided over by the unrighteous judge.

"Dare any of you, having a matter against another, go to law before the unrighteous, and not before the saints? Do

you not know that the saints will judge the world? And if the world will be judged by you, are you unworthy to judge the smallest matter?... If then you have judgments concerning things pertaining to this life, do you appoint those who are least esteemed by the church to judge? I say this to your shame. Is it so, that there is not a wise man among you, not even one, who will be able to judge between the brethren? But brother goes to law against brother, and that before unbelievers!" 1 Corinthians 6:1-6.

There are currently many cases before the maintenance courts, domestic violence etc. where Christians have taken each other to courts. Most of these cases have not even been heard in the church but are already with the courts. Paul's advice to the church is this,

"Now therefore, it is already an utter failure for you that you go to law against one another. Why do you not rather accept wrong? Why do you not rather let yourselves be cheated? No, you yourselves do wrong and cheat, and you do these things to your brethren!" verse 7-8.

It is therefore imperative that structures be constituted within the church that would deal with dispute resolutions in light of the growing number of cases before the courts brought by brethren against one another.

In a letter to Timothy, Paul gave him advice on how he needed to establish and constitute the structure of the church. He puts emphasis on the qualities of the leadership and deacons because these would play a major role in dispute resolutions as their lives would be exemplary (1 Timothy 3) to others.

> *"Be diligent to present yourself approved to God, a worker who does not need to be ashamed, rightly dividing the word of truth...In humility correcting those who are in opposition, if God perhaps will grant them repentance, so that they may know the truth, and that they may come to their senses and escape the snare of the devil, having been taken captive by him to do his will" 2 Timothy 2:15, 25- 26.*

It is therefore imperative that these conditions be considered when such committees are established. Paul also urged us to consider the public conduct of members of the committee,

> *"Moreover, he must have a good testimony among those who are outside, lest he fall into reproach and the snare of the devil" (1 Timothy 3:7).*

One thing is for certain here, that there is a need for such committee to be constituted and the church would do well if she establishes it. As for the protocol given to us by our Lord Jesus regarding the handling of differences, the scriptures are very clear regarding the path to be followed and we will do well to follow this process in our daily dealings with our fellow brethren.

Seek justice and not victory

"Righteousness and justice are the foundation of Your throne..." Psalms 89:14

As Christians, our duty is towards the Christ first and foremost. We are the ambassadors of His kingdom. This is the reason why our God delivered us from the kingdom of darkness and translated us into the kingdom of the Son of His love. We are to advance the kingdom of Christ at all costs and aggressively. Scripture already told that Satan is angry and he knows that his time is short. His anger is against human beings in general and Christians in particular (Revelation 12:13 & 17).

The prophet Isaiah tells us that to the increase of His government and peace there shall be no end. This kingdom has to advance and we are here to do just that. Having said that, we need to remember that the reason why this kingdom cannot be shaken is because of its strong foundations, righteousness and Justice. These two have become a very rare commodity in the world today. Not only in families but society in general. Daily we hear stories of bribes and injustices affecting our people.

The Lord Jesus left us to be the lights off the world. As long as we are here, the world should not be   in darkness. It is unfortunate that we who are the ambassadors of His kingdom are the ones today guilty of the injustices and unrighteousness in our relations with one another. Unforgiveness has raised its ugly head and prevailing because we have deviated from kingdom principles thus exposing our foundations.

The pattern has been revealed to us, righteousness and justice are to be the foundation in all our dealings with one another. The moment we deviate from this, we begin to stand on shaky ground. Every time we have an argument or differences with one another, we should always strive for justice not victory. I was taught this by the Lord during many heated arguments I would have with my wife. It was during one of those moments that the Lord taught me this. He said to me I should always strive for objectivity, seeking to advance His justice and not my ego. Often times, I had argued for the sake of arguing because I wanted to win the argument for my ego not because it was the right thing. I know this is common in all the relationships. It is very rare that we advance justice. "A ka ntlwaela" (sic), we say and this attitude has landed many relationships in trouble leading to separation at times.

> "He has shown you, O man; what is good. And what does the Lord require of you, but to do justly, to love mercy and to walk humbly with your God" Micah 6:8

For the sake of the point, I want to drive home, allow me to replace God here with spouse/friend etc. The Lord requires us to do justly, meaning to act with justice at all times. We should never attempt to exalt ourselves over others especially our spouses or people we relate to. Justice always has to drive our actions. The other thing here is that scripture says He has shown us what is good. It is not good to deny others justice. If I am wrong, I should man up and accept my wrongs. It is foolishness and detrimental to our relationships to argue for the sake of wanting to win the argument. Such behavior leads to bitterness which is the beginning of unforgiveness.

Our dealings with our spouses and by extension those we relate to, must be truthful and always mindful of their feelings. Bitterness and unforgiveness is the ground we should never cultivate. Let us advance justice and seek to legislate justice at all times. There are a lot of injustices and atrocities being committed in the society and we being the light should stand against. But we must first start with ourselves. There is no need for the in-laws to mistreat their makoti (daughter-in-law) and cause her to be bitter. There is no need for the husband to cultivate that ground, no need at all for the children to be caused to be bitter by their parents. We can avoid this and must avoid it. Advance justice in all your dealings. Don't do things by force. Remember, God sees the heart and the pain of your spouse and will demand justice from you.

The second part of the foundation from the above scriptures is righteousness which simply means right standing with God. I think if we can be considerate of this scripture and our desire to be positioned right with God, we will solve many unnecessary conflicts. It is very key to seek to maintain our standing in God regardless of what we may be experiencing.

The Lord Jesus could have dealt with Jews harshly. He fed them, raised their dead, healed their sic and delivered their oppressed but they still crucified Him. Instead of being bitter and sought revenge, He cried to the Father to forgive them. There are two reasons to this, first is that He wanted His right position with God. Any action other than what He did would have been out of anger and resentment. His righteousness would have been compromised and that would have been thwarted His resurrection. God made Him to be sin (2 Cor 5:21), He never sinned.

Second reason is that He knew that they didn't know what they were doing. The people were convinced they were doing the right thing and justice by crucifying Him. They were convinced by their lack of knowledge and discernment that He was teaching false doctrine as it was contrary to their belief in the Law of Moses. The people could not discern between their left and their right (Jonah 4:11) and what righteousness would have been if this was their condition? What justice would have been served against someone who doesn't know what they are doing?

Do you know that many couples are punished for the things they are not even aware they are wrong? How many of our relations become sour because we feel we were ill-treated by people who are not even aware they have wronged us? It is for this reason that we should always put our emotions aside and analyze the situation thoroughly. Interrogate their actions and questions their motives and loyalty. This should be the barometer of knowing whether what they did was spiteful or innocent. It is difficult for someone who loves you to deliberately and intentionally hurt you.

Be merciful

".... Mercy and truth go before Your face" Psalms 89:14

The 'b' part of the scripture above says mercy and truth go before your face. Every human being has benefited from the above scripture. Given, there are still many who haven't come to the light and receive the free gift of mercy of the Lord however those of us who are saved are the beneficiaries of God's mercy towards humanity.

Two things are clear from the above scripture namely, mercy and truth and both go before His face. This means He is aware of them and they inform His decisions and actions. Had it not been for the mercy o the Lord which is before is face, humanity would have been left to its destruction forever. Had it not been for the mercy of the Lord, you and I would not have been saved.

"The steadfast love of the Lord never ceases, His mercies never come to an end; they are new every morning, great is your faithfulness" Lamentations 3:22-23 (ESV)

The mercies of the Lord are given anew as a daily dose and we being His servants should apply the same measure. Scripture says freely we have received and freely we should give (Mathew 10:8). Mercy says even though you are wrong, but I will soften my heart and look at you favorably. Just as we need the mercies daily, we should also understand we need to be merciful towards others daily.

James tells us that mercy triumph over judgment (James 2:13). It does not matter how much we have judged one another for whatever reason, when we introduce mercy in the situation, it always triumphs over judgments. Regardless of how a person has behaved or is behaving because they are bitter and unforgiving, we need to deploy the weapon of mercy over the situation and arrest the behavior. Mercy is victorious and a daily dose like medicine will go a long way to stabilizing our relation.

> *"For judgement is without mercy to the one who has shown no mercy" James 2:13*

On the other hand, we need to be careful that we don't harden our hearts towards our relations. If we are not merciful as the scripture commands us, we run the risk of being judged mercilessly by our Lord Jesus. While we are doing service to our relations by being merciful, we shouldn't do ourselves de- service by withholding mercy when it is in our power to show one.

> *"Do not withhold good from those who deserve it when it's in your power to help them" Proverbs 3:27 (NLT)*

Hang on before you say but they don't deserve it. None of us deserve the mercy of God. We are saved by grace and grace alone through faith in Christ Jesus. It is for this reason that we daily approach the throne of grace that we may obtain mercy and find grace just as we need it. Without the mercy of God, we are nothing therefore let us show kindness to one another especially to those who needs it.

Act truthfully

"…. Mercy and truth go before Your face"
Psalms 89:14

Truth remains the most attacked of God's characters. Everywhere in society through various channels including media, the truth has come under tremendous pressure. Commissions after commissions are being established in our country to deal with the scourge of graft and corruption because people were not truthful in their dealings. Many have been exposed for falsifying their qualifications and thus gaining advantage in positions they did not qualify for because of not being truthful in their dealings.

"And you shall now the truth, and the truth shall
make you free" John 8:32

This is a very direct and liberating statement. It is only the truth that makes us free. It is very critical that in our relational dealings, we need to be truthful at all times. At some stage we have string of arguments and fighting over money with my wife and I couldn't understand what was happening. After some time, I decided to enquire of the Lord what was happening and how I could resolve the impasse. The Lord told me to be honest in my financial dealings with my wife.

I used to withdraw money from the house without telling her and I felt justified in doing that because I have been saving while she was spending her portion. The company we were working for was giving us housing subsidy and I had requested her to contribute that amount towards our bond repayments but she refused. I felt that due to this, I was entitled to the savings as I was paying above the required amount and had lots of savings as a result.

My discussion within the Lord opened my mind. According to His standard, that was dishonesty since I was not being truthful to my wife. Christ is the way, the truth and the life (John 14:6). He says mercy and truth go before His face. The truth is there is a lot of dishonesty especially among couples when it comes to money. I have spoken to several women who confessed to having their savings account which their spouse knew nothing about. That is the breeding ground for bitterness.

You can imagine the man working very hard, denying himself some of the things he really wants in life, for his family unknown to him that the wife is secretly keeping some stash. He is borrowing money yet there is money in the house kept in the secret bank account. How will this man feel when he finds out?

I spoke to a young lady who refuses to contribute anything in the house because her husband is working. He is supporting her son (whom she came within their marriage) and yet she is saving all her money secretly. Even when he is struggling supporting three families (his own, his mother and mother-in-law as the boy stays with his grandmother), she refuses to assist. This is recipe for disaster. There is no truth in that marriage and a huge door has been opened for the enemy to devour

> *".... The gates of your land are wide open or your enemies..."*
> *Nahum 3:13*

Such marriage will constantly endure attacks. The couple is always arguing over petty issues. There is no peace. This door must be closed and the enemy be kept out. Truth makes us free. Let us strive to be and act truthfully in our dealings, our activities within our homes and marriages. We can stop a lot of unnecessary arguments and strive once this is done. It is not worth it.

> *"If we say that we have fellowship with Him, and walk in darkness, we lie and do not practice the truth"* *1 John 1:6*

There it is! Jesus is the truth and we cannot relate to Him while walking in darkness. John says this is tantamount to lying and not practicing the truth. Family, we need the fellowship with Christ. Let us come clean, be honest and truthful in our dealings. Deal with the person who is experiencing bitterness and unforgiveness in truth. The truth will make them free and also remove the heavy burden from your shoulders. You don't need this, and they don't need this bitterness and unforgiveness. Stay in the liberty with which Christ set us free (Galatians 5:1).

Cover the multitude of sins

"Above all, love each other deeply, because love
covers over a multitude of sins" I Peter 4:8

Remember this person is hurting. Most of the things they say and do, they have no idea what they are doing. In their sober mind and state, they will not say or do them. Deal with them dealing with a weaker vessel. Learn to cover the multitude of their sins. Ignore what they say and do. Don't take it personal.

You see the reason why God did not destroy the city of Nineveh, even though he had told Jonah that He was going to destroy it, is that He noticed that the hundred and twenty thousand people in that city could not discern between their let and their right. This is what He told Jonah when he protested,

"And should I not pity Nineveh, that great city, in which
are more than one hundred and twenty thousand persons,
who cannot discern between their right hand and their left
– and much livestock?" Johan 4:11

Many of us are the Jonas today towards our relations. We have no tolerance to their weaknesses, bitterness, anger and unforgiveness due to our preconceived ideas. We have chosen to cut the branches hoping for the tree to die instead of dealing with and cutting the roots. The removal of the roots will ensure that this tree never grows again. Don't deal with the symptoms but address the problem with love. Ensure that you act with love at all times. God did when dealing with the Ninevites. We are in a position to reciprocate and do what the Lord has done. Cover the multitudes of sins. Don't count the sins against them.

Look this is easier said than done. I know because I have been in this situation before with my wife. The combination of many unattended queries, concerns and challenges resulted in her being seriously bitter. It was very difficult to deal with her and she made sure that I feel what she was feeling. Our home changed to a house. I would spend time away and only came in when I was sure they are asleep. It was not possible to have a decent conversation as a couple. Few minutes into the discussions, then we are fighting again. It became so bad that it was now even physical.

I asked the Lord for help and this was not once. The Lord gave me grace and each time we experience the episode, I would ask the Lord for grace to endure and another grace to forgive. I have learnt to cover the multitude of sins by just asking the Lord for grace.

"And God is able to make all grace abound to you; so that always having all sufficiency in everything, you may have

an abundance for every good deed" 2 Cor 9:8 (NASB)

Please note! You can never deal with bitterness and unforgiving person by yourself using the worldly means. It is impossible. You need the grace of the Lord. You have to ask and ask abundantly. That is the only way you are going to be able to deal with this. Bitter people are unpredictable and their moods fluctuate. One look at you revives all the hidden hatred and from there anything can happen. Unless the Lord gives you His grace abundantly, you would not be able to do good deed towards the person.

> *"And the God of all grace, who called you to His eternal glory in Christ, after you have suffered a little while, will Himself restore you and make you strong, firm and steadfast" 1 Peter 5:10*

God loves to give His children good gifts. Grace is a good gift in the hour of need. Go for it and receive it abundantly from the God of all grace.

Ask for peace from the Lord

"Peace, I leave with you, My peace I give to you, not as the world gives do, I give to you." John 14:27

The Lord Jesus was clear that in the world, we will have challenges/tribulations. The situations and circumstances will be so demanding that without His peace, we run the risk of implosion. I have learnt through many practical experiences to ask not only grace but His peace as well. Many times, I found myself pushed to the limit, the man in me wanting to manifest himself to the world.

As indicated in the previous pointers, bitter people are unpredictable. Their mood swings easily from one extreme to the other extreme without any warning. It becomes very difficult to adjust between the two extremes and often you are caught unprepared. In those instances, the Holy Spirit taught me to ask for peace of the Lord. Boy, I tell you. This has worked wonders for me and helped me to adjust without losing control of my emotions. The moment you ask for this peace, the Lord grants and although you may be in the middle of an argument or heated exchanges, this peace calms your nerves right there and there.

The peace of the world is conditional and dependent on various factors. But the Lord Jesus gives us the peace that surpasses all human understanding (Philippians 4:8). You cannot comprehend it because in the midst of turmoil of volcanic magnitude, you find yourself relaxed as if there are no earthquakes around.

I understand when Paul says this peace surpasses human understanding. My heart was indeed guarded and I urge you to try this and watch the Prince of peace at work.

"And the peace of God, which surpasses all understanding, will guard your hearts and minds through Christ" *Philippians 4:7*

One thing you need to avoid is tuning in to the same modulation as the person. When their volume is loud, ask for this peace so that you maintain calm and avoid unexpected actions. My grandmother always advised me to always avoid taking any action while in the state of anger. She said such actions have dire and unintended consequences which are always regrettable.

Our Lord Jesus is the Prince of peace and He said wisdom is known by her children (Luke 7:35). This means we must be prepared to sow in peace at any time. We cannot be found wanting, let your wisdom be vindicated by your children (fruits/actions). Let us follow in His footsteps. He spoke and made provision for this peace because He knew in the world, we will need this peace while navigating through the terrain of life.

"And those who are peacemakers will plant seeds of peace and reap a harvest of righteousness" James 3:18

Let us sow the seed of peace. Promote peace, pursue peace with every person (Hebrews 12:14), ask for the peace of the Lord to fill and guard your heart. We need this. You need this. As ambassadors of the kingdom of the Christ, we owe it to our Master to pursue peace with all men. It is for our own good and will help calm the situation and storms we often find ourselves in. Maintaining calm will calm the brewing storm and divert the anger hence the desperate need for the peace of the Lord.

Finally, in all your endeavors and doings, please Don't give up on them. They need you more than they can imagine. They may not be aware of this due to the emotions that have clouded their judgement at the time but given opportunity and space to calm down and reflect, they will see and appreciate what you have done for them.

Have compassion

"When He saw the crowds, He was deeply moved with compassion for them, because they were troubled and helpless, like sheep without a shepherd" Mathew 9:36 (ISV)

Compassion was the cornerstone of our Lord Jesus Christ throughout His earthly ministry. Every healing and deliverance that He did was out of compassion for the people. The above scripture shows us the depth of His compassion towards the people. He likened them to sheep without a shepherd. According to His analysis of their condition, they were lost and in a state. This state resulted in them being troubled and helpless.

There is no feeling as painful and frustrating like the feeling of being defeated and helpless. Once the person enters this state, they lose their vitality. Their face loses its spark and even their demeanor and appearance look defeated. Because of what is happening inside, even how the person looks outside changes. Their face is sorrowful because the troubled heart and spirit.

"A merry heart makes a cheerful countenance, but by sorrow of the heart the spirit is broken" Proverbs 15:13

The heart is troubled and as such their spirit is broken. This will affect their countenance. It is easy to pick up a person in the crowd who has a sorrowful heart by just looking at their countenance. Truth be told, such a person is troubled and helpless. They need someone to assist them. It is easier for them to end up committing suicide because they are helpless. We need to show deep compassion towards and help them from that perspective. Their spirit is already broken and only compassion will help. We need to be considerate and hold their hands, be compassionate while assuring them of our love for them. They need to feel loved and see our actions reflecting this love.

Love is powerful and is able to break every barrier no matter how strong it may be. The feeling of compassion towards the people came as a result of His deeper love for humanity. Acts of kindness will go a long way to assisting the person whose spirit is broken. Be nice and kind. Show deep care for the person and avoid harsh words. Remember they are troubled and feel helpless. They need extra care and that we are careful around them considering always the fact that they are unpredictable.

I believe that what made Jesus to cry before raising Lazarus was the state the people were in. He saw people troubled and helpless because they were defeated by death. He was moved with compassion for them. Like the Lord Jesus, our ministering to them must be driven and inspired by compassion. They are not themselves and as such need understanding than judgement.

"A soft answer turns away wrath, but a harsh word stirs up anger" proverbs 15:1

Avoid unnecessary arguments at all cost. Better to move away for a time than to remain and risk the possibility of speaking harshly to them. And when you speak, be mindful of your words no matter how much you feel you are being pushed. Let your soft answer turn away wrath. They are already in a state and you don't want to exacerbate the situation. Be there; continuously assure them of your love and care. Listen if they want to speak. Don't interrupt when they speak. Ask them to propose solution or path to be followed for their healing.

Remember, you are there for them not the other way round. Make them the center of focus and attention and demonstrate understanding. Allow them to lead the conversation while you constantly nod to show that you are giving them full attention. Compassion, compassion and compassion. That is what is needed. Acts of kindness will always go a long way in taming wayward behavior and drive aware anxiety.

> *"Anxiety in the heart of man causes depression, but a good word makes it glad" Proverbs 12:25*

One of the many fruits of bitterness and unforgiveness is loss of trust and where there is not trust, love fades. The absence of love or perception that one is not loved will results in anxiety and fear. Scripture tells us perfect love cast out fear (1 John 5:18). It says that there is no fear in love hence it is absolutely critical that we must consistently affirm our love for them. This will gradually give them assurance resulting in trust being restored. When there is trust, there is assurance which will results in love and a merry heart and rejuvenated spirit. Love is a good word and it will bring gladness. These are derivatives of compassion.

Unforgiveness and bitterness leads to multiple personality syndromes.

"When he saw Jesus from afar, he ran and worshipped Him" Mark 5:6

There was a man from the country of Gadarenes who met Jesus when He came out of the boat. He had an unclean spirit (demon).

"who had his dwelling among the tombs, and no one could bind him, not even with chains, because he had often been bound with shackles and chains. And the chains had been pulled apart by him, and the shackles broken in pieces; neither could anyone tame him. And always night and day, he was in the mountains and in the tombs, crying out and cutting himself with stones" Mark 5:3-5

Scripture shows us several things about the unusual personality of this man. First, he was dwellings among the tombs. Our language will say he was dwelling at the graveyard. Right there, this is spooky and a taboo. Second, he had an unusual strength to break chains and shackles. This is uncommon among the children of men. Third, he was crying out. This means he didn't like his condition and was crying for help. He needed someone to reach out and help him. Fourth, he was cutting himself with stones. He was hurting himself. No normal human being would deliberate harm or put himself in harm's way. This is strange and unusual.

Although his actions were deliberate, however it was not voluntary. This is first confirmed by his crying out and secondly by him running to Jesus and worshipping Him. Demons are at war with Christ and would not voluntarily run to Him and worship. The man had multiple personality.

At one moment, he was hurting himself and another, he was crying for help. Demons had taken over and were influencing his actions at times and not always. The slim window opportunity he got; he ran to Jesus. His running to Jesus was a sign of a man desperate for help. Demons would never run to Jesus for help. So, we can clearly see the signs of multiple personality playing out in the life of this man.

Bitter and unforgiving people run the risk of

experiencing multiple personality syndromes. One moment, the demons take over and lead them to an undesirable action and the next moment they are sober and unaware of their actions. They can hurt their child in a moment of rage and then cry from the feeling of remorse and despondency due to what they have done. Their own children fear them because they don't know what they are dealing with and what their actions would be next.

I first had an encounter with this spirit in a church I had visited in Braamfischer, Soweto. A certain couple had come to church and the pastor through the spirit of discernment noticed the multiple personality in the woman. She commanded the spirit to demonstrate to the church what it does   to the husband at home. In a moment of rage, she began to roar and breaking things. The pastor then rebuked the demons and asked the husband what was happening.

He told the church what she does at home, how she would suddenly stand up and bath with the intention of going to town but the net moment she can't remember what she was doing and why she bathed. He further indicated how out of rage, she would break the utensils and cutleries only to feel bad afterwards.

Since then, I have leant to be mindful of multiple personality. It is absolute critical that you are mindful of your proximity to such a person to avoid unnecessary casualties or even fatalities. Please note, they have absolutely no idea of what they have done and why they have done it. Demons had taken over their mind and actions for a period to bring confusion and strive with their relations.

> "The thief does not come except to steal, and to kill and to destroy" John 10:10

The intention and purpose of multiple personalityis to advance the above verse. They want to steal the livelihood of a person. If that doesn't happen, they will attempt and at times succeed in killing him/ her. Still if that doesn't succeed, they will destroy the person and their relation/s. They hate human relationship with a passion and seek to destroy it at every level, husband and wife, children with their parents and even children with children, what we refer as sibling rivalry. The person with multiple personality needs deliverance. The natural response would be to lock them in a mental hospital for   life however this is not a solution though as this condition can be resolved.

Our Lord Jesus Christ demonstrated that to us clearly with the man of Gadarenes. He cast the devils out of him and the man was restored fully and immediately. There was no injection, medicine or psychiatric evaluations, just pure gospel of the kingdom, deliverance.

"For He said to him, „Come out of the man, unclean spirit!" Then they came to Jesus, and

saw the one who had been demon-possessed and had the legion, sitting and clothed and in his right mind. And they were afraid" Mark 5:6 ;15

Once the Lord Jesus addressed the unclean spirit, the man was delivered and his condition restored. His sanity returned to him and he was no longer a threat to the community and himself. The same situation can and must happen to our relations who have multiple personality so that they are free indeed and no longer a threat to themselves and others.

Address the demonic opportunist

"Be sober, be vigilant; because your adversary the devil walks about like a roaring lion, seeking whom he may devour" 1 Peter 5:8

Life is spiritual and everything on earth has a spiritual connotation. Once the person becomes bitter and unforgiving, they open doors for demonic influence. There are unclean spirits lacking around looking for a body to inhabit. They are following their master's instructions. He is roaring like a lion, seeing whom he may devour and what a fertile is the person who is bitter.

The spirit will take advantage of the feeling and manipulate their behavior and actions from here. You will no longer be dealing with one character but multiple personalities. This is a difficult situation to deal if you lack the spirit of discernment. The personality interchange in the blink of an eye and before you know it, you are no longer speaking   to your spouse but a demonic personality.

The things that come out of their mouth are foul and destructive. Be very careful when dealing with this and avoid close proximity. They turn to pick up a fight too quick and can use anything to hurt you with. Remember this is no longer a person but a demon who hates human beings with a passion.

The case in point is of that young man who was brought by his father to the disciples to deliver him.

They could not and later when Jesus came, the father narrated the story to him,

"And often he has thrown him both into the fire and into the water to destroy him..." Mark 9:22

Demons have only one mission on earth: destroy as many people as possible and they are looking for opened doors they can use to advance and execute their plans. Prolonged bitterness and unforgiveness is an invitation for demonic take over. Once they are in, they invite other demons to come in and afflict the person. The unforgiveness spirit becomes the door keeper and unless the Spirit of the Lord reveal this through the spirit of discernment, it is hard for their other demons to come.

I once was praying for a woman and the Lord said she has problem of unforgiveness. The woman was afflicted by many sicknesses. The Lord said we should ask her to forgive the people who hurt her and renounce unforgiveness. When I said this, she screamed because the spirit of unforgiveness has been exposed. I commanded the spirit to back off and asked her to do what the Lord commanded. Once this was done, she was not only delivered but was also healed of other infirmities she had.

The gatekeeper must be dealt with first before addressing any other. I have learnt that most sicknesses or illnesses are actually as a result of unforgiveness. Once unforgiveness is dealt with, the person's health improves. The sicknesses and other afflictions are but the smoke screen taking advantage of the door opened by unforgiveness. Many people are spending lots of money with physicians on sicknesses caused by bitterness and unforgiveness. You don't need doctors to deal with a spirit. Demon spirit will bow to the power of the Holy Spirit called anointing. It is there to break the jokes (Isaiah 10:27). You need this, not injection.

All people that have unforgiveness are under demonic attack and will manifest other infirmities in their bodies. They spend their fortunes on physicians without success. Physical solutions for a spiritual problem will only yield temporary relief. Whatever injection or medication one is taking to address infirmity is powerless against a demonic force. Address and shut the open door of unforgiveness for a permanent solution. Demons don't like living their comfort zone within the human body, they call it their house.

> "When an evil spirit goes out a person, it travels over dry country looking for a place to rest. If it can't find one, it says to itself, „I will go back to my house"" Luke 11:24

No human being should be a home to a demon. Nothing good will come out of that. Demons hate human beings, they are livid. Their anger and hatred can be best described by the suffering our Lord Jesus Christ went through on the Cross of Calvary.

They don't like dry place because there they cannot unleash their wickedness, misery and afflictions. Only in human beings can they best manifest their wicked agenda and activities. They have no mercy and as such we should not tolerate them.

Do not open the door. If it opens, close it quickly through forgiveness and repentance. The legion in Mark 5 who went into pigs requested Christ to allow them to remain in the region. Why do you think Christ allowed them? He could have cast them out of the person and then the area but He didn't. These were actors and not gatekeepers. His focus was on the big price, Satan himself. Driving this out would not have a permanent effect, as long as the god of this age (their master Satan) was not cast out; they still had legal right over the territory.

In the same way, as long as the unforgivess spirit is not driven out, the other demons have legal ground over the person and are thus permitted by this law to exploit the situation to their benefit. Do away with the bitterness and unforgiveness, and then there would be no legal standing for the enemy over your life. They need our help. Make them see reason by first praying for them, for the Lord Jesus to open their eyes to the sin of unforgiveness. They can't do this by themselves.

"Brethren, if a man is overtaken in any trespass, you who are spiritual restore such a one in a spirit of gentleness, considering yourself lest you also be tempted. Bear one another's burdens and so fulfill the law of Christ" Galatians 6:1-2

Let us unpack the above scripture. First, we need to understand that a person with the spirit of unforgiveness has been overtaken in a trespass. The Lord commanded us to forgive one another even as he has forgiven us (Ephesians 4:32). Secondly, the Lord commands us who are sober to help restore such a person. We are not to fold our arms and let them be. We have to restore them. Thirdly, our actions must be done in the spirit of gentleness being careful lest we also be overtaken.

The word used here is tempted. How do we get tempted? By ignoring the facts that they are troubled and helpless and instead refusing to forgive them as well. This will defeat the whole purpose of trying to help. Fourthly, our Lord exhorts us to bear their burden. Let them not carry the load alone but reach out to them and help. The load of bitterness, resentment and unforgiveness is too heavy and as such unbearable. That is why it has impact on one's spirit as well as countenance. It changes even the pigmentation of one's skin. A bitter person is sick and need help. Forgiveness will be a pill to them.

Lastly the bible says by doing this, we shall fulfil the laws of Christ. This law of Christ is the law of love. We love Christ because He first loved us (1 John 5:19). He didn't bitter towards even when we rejected Him. We crucified Him and hated Him for loving us yet despite all these treatments we were and are still giving Him, he chose to ask the Father to forgive us. He mentioned that we do not know what we were and are doing (Luke 23:34). This is the choice we have to make today towards our relations, forgive them because they don't know what they are doing.

Part 4

Testimony

Testimony 1

"I, even I, am He who blots out your transgressions for My own sake; and I will not remember your sins" Isaiah 43:25

It took me a long time after I became to fully understand the meaning of the above passage. I could not comprehend why the Lord would say He blots out my transgression for His own sake. God never sins and thus He can never be affected by sin. Why would He then blot out my transgressions for His own sake and not my sake? I would have understood better if He had said for my sake not His sake because I am the one who needs to be forgiven not Him. Well, this was until I had to learn that there is a need to forgive others for my own sake. And boy, I learned the hard way.

All the days my life, I had never struggled with forgiveness. God had particularly graced me sufficiently with the humble heart to forgiven. I would forgive people easily. During my early years as a Christian, a very close member of my family did me wrong, there was a funeral of the husband and they told my mother that there is no money for burial. My mother then requested me to step in and assist. I did not have sufficient money and went for an overdraft on my credit card to cover the costs of the funeral. After the funeral, I was indebted and had to work overtime to repay the debt. A month or so later after the funeral, I received a call from my mother. The son of the relative had called mama that morning to notify her of the family's greed. According to him, the family had a burial society but lied to mama regarding lack of funds so that I can do the funeral while they cash in the society money. He only confessed because while they shared the money among themselves, they refused to share with him.

This was very painful for me as I had put my life on hold to assist the children financially to build their lives. I was also very close to the relative   and wouldn't have imagined, not in single day that she could ever treat me like that since she had seen the efforts, I had taken to try to assist her children. Although I was hurting, I chose the path of forgiveness and decided to move on. I was focused on my relationship with the Lord and wanted nothing to interfere with that. I knew if I did not forgive, this would have opened a door of unforgiveness and attracted demonic attacks and I didn't want that to happen to me. I had set my eyes like a flint to the Lord and that was all that mattered.

I continued to assist the next couple of years. Unfortunately, despite all the support I gave and financial injection in their lives, none of them took advantage of the situation and build their lives for the better. After sometime and amid many meetings I had with them, I decided to withdraw my support and only assist as and when I could.

Testimony 2

"I, even I, am He who blots out your transgressions for My own sake; and I will not remember your sins" Isaiah 43:25

By this time, I had been married for 12 years. The year was 2015 and 3 years earlier, I had opened a can of worms I shouldn't have by trying to write the wrong I had committed years before I could meet my wife. I had a relationship with a young lady whom I was told later that she became pregnant. I had not seen her for almost 9 months since we last met when I came to Pretoria for a course. I made efforts to come and see the baby. Her sister had told me though that the child could not have been mine since, the sis had run away from home and stayed for months with another young man (adolescent stage).

I called her and she told me that the child was mine. I took a train to Pretoria and visited her house to see the baby. I left the house unconvinced and never made contacts with her. Before I got married, I explained to my fiancé about the whole situation and the choice I made at the time. Fast forward, when I was 11 years in marriage, my dad passed away and I attended his unreal (he was not married to my mom) and met several of my siblings from different mothers. There were 5 of us from different mothers and mom told me of the 6ᵗʰ who was older than me.

I began to do introspection as by then I was dealing with the bloodline issues. I was my father's son and his blood was in me.

What if I also abandoned my daughter those many years, seeing now so many of father's children? I decided to pursue the matter to establish if the child was mine. Now, I had two options in doing this. The first choice was to involve my wife and work on this together or do some preliminary investigations and tell her later when I had gathered sufficient information. I chose the latter, and when my wife found out before I could tell her, my house became a war zone.

Despite the efforts of trying to resolve this amicable, the situation and tension escalated. My wife saw the child as a threat and even though we were having 2 children by then, she was not willing to have a stranger come into her space. The thought of that child drove her mad and she became very bitter to a point where our peace became the thing of the past. I decided to abandon the quest for the sake of peace but the bitterness was deep. According to her, I had betrayed her when I chose to investigate the issue the child.

We had countless meetings with families, friends, pastors, social workers and even psychologists but all the meetings did not yield any results. She had built a wall and things were going to be done her way or the highway. The situation took a serious toll on her health, and soon she was in and out of hospitals. I had opened a pandora box and unleashed a creature I was now unable to tame. Our relationship suffered tremendously and affected every other level of relations we had with other people. Her friends were no longer our friends and my friends the same. Each one of them had their own opinion and it was not helping the situation.

Two years later, the child called me and wanted to be part of my life. I had abandoned the matter for the sake of my marriage and my wife's health but now we had to deal with it once again. I explained to my wife reluctantly about the call and the roof came down once again. By this time, she was on medication and constantly visiting doctors. The pain was deep, and because she was not willing to let go, her health deteriorated. She hated the child with a passion, and this affected other interventions to resolve the problem.

I had requested the mother of the child to do paternity test as earlier agreed but my wife was threatened by the results. She didn't want the child to have any relations with our children and made this clear to the child's mother. Their conversations were also volatile and didn't end well. The family had agreed that I should pursue the matter for resolution by insisting on the paternity test but my wife interfered with this by calling the mother and telling the child would not be welcomed in her house.

This situation impacted our ministry very much. By this time, we were running the church and my wife stopped attending. We had only one car which was registered in her name. My car was stolen some years before and the Lord had told me not to buy one until He released me. Running a ministry became hard and often I will carry musical instruments and walk to the church when the car was parked at home. My wife would often come but only occasionally. Soon, she stopped the children as well and our relationship suffered. She was on a warpath and wanted everyone to know.

Despite all the efforts as resoling this, nothing came through and I began to bitter towards her. The treatment was very harsh and embarrassing at times. Bitterness engulfed me, and I lost vitality. Soon my health also deteriorated. My blood pressure would shoot sky high and I was put on a pill. I remember one day I was taking the tables when the Lord asked me a question, you and the tablets? I was embarrassed and ashamed that I had become so weak. My prayer suffered so was my fasting. I gained weight due to stress which also caused the high blood pressure. I was angry with my wife and it was affecting me all round.

"A merry heart makes a cheerful countenance, but by sorrow of the heart the spirit is broken" Proverbs 15:13

I was a broken man and this affected not only the ministry but my performance at work also began to suffer as well. I lost confidence and would literally freeze when women scream at me. I had serious anger issues and would often shout at innocent people over small issues. I was using a taxi to go work even though my wife and I were working opposite buildings. She did not allow me in her car. She refused to forgive me for the child issue.

The paternity was later done and results came back negative. I asked my wife to let go so that we may start afresh, but the impact of bitterness and unforgiveness stayed with her for some time. She never really forgave me and would always ensure that I know her feelings every time she had to go to the doctor. After realizing the impact bitterness was having on me, I asked the Lord to help me. He gave me the grace and helped me to forgive and forget.

I started by forgiving myself, then my wife and lastly the mother of the child. She had affected my family tremendously with her lies. She told the child I was the father even though she knew the truth, the father had died soon after the child was born. I was a teacher of the Word, an intercessor as well as a pastor. I should have known the danger of allowing bitterness in my heart. My ministry had suffered and we had lost a lot of good people that should not have left. The finances of the church had also suffered and we lost the opportunity of receiving the land parcel from government because I was not focused. To date, we have no land of our own and we are still re-building from the impact.

Although I had resisted the temptation of divorce that came from many advisors, however the impact on the grace upon my life was too deep. I had lost far much more than I could have imagined. I lost the assignment the Lord gave me to establish the Council of Church Elders in Limpopo. Although we managed to establish it however, I pulled back despite the Lord advising that I shouldn't. The Council became dormant and never achieved the impact it should have had. I also lost my personal intercessory ministry, MSM which the Lord assigned back in 2007 during my 40 days of fasting. This also saw me withdraw from the national prayer network, SAPMC which I was part of the founding fathers.

I am only starting to regain some of the initiatives now for example writing. I had books which were left attended which I was supposed to have finished long time ago. In addition, I was working on films which also had to be abandoned due to the stress. Brethren, bitterness and unforgiveness are very dangerous and have far reaching consequences than we could ever imagine.

Do your level best to stay away from this. It is not worth it. I am a witness and I have lost far much. It will only take God's grace to fully restore me and all I have lost of His assignments upon my life.

Testimony 3

"I, even I, am He who blots out your transgressions for My own sake; and I will not remember your sins" Isaiah 43:25

This testimony is from a lady whom I know very well whom I will call Jane for the purpose of writing. Jane has been married for over 5 years and is blessed with two children. She had a very good relationship with her husband whom she met and stayed with many years before they decided to get married. The delay was mutual due to other commitments each one had to their families.

Like many men, the husband had relationships before meeting her. Two of those relationships yielded children although he decided on both occasions not to marry the ladies. After meeting Jane, the man settled down and later committed to her through marriage and matrimonial celebration. But that time, they had already been blessed with a child.

Before the wedding, the mother of one of the children would make funny remarks but she didn't take it to heart, assuming she was saying things out of spite because he chose her and not the other woman. It would be years later when the man became very sick. The family did not know what the cause of the sickness was. The wife was not working at the time, took care of him even though the in-laws decided to take their son.

They suspected that she had bewitched him, which was not the case at all.

After the man regained strength and was back at his house, the wife discovered the truth on the cause of the near fatal sickness. The man was HIV positive and has been for a while and had chosen to keep the secret away from his wife. The news broke her and affected their relationship for a long time. The once beautiful home became a battlefield. She made a decision never to honor her matrimonial duties in as far as the husband is concerned.

The last lady the husband had left before getting married to her knew about the condition hence the strange remarks she would make whenever she opportunity presented itself. The man had been positive and known about it even before he could propose to Jane yet despite this, he chose to remain quiet and never shared the news with her. As a couple, they had engaged in unprotected sexual intercourse, while he knew very well, he was positive. It wasn't clear whether he did this deliberately or he honestly did not accept that he was positive. I know many people including a member of my family who died of Aids after refusing to accept that he was positive. He believed with all his heart despite the tests and results that he was bewitched.

Jane lived with the pain of betrayal for a long time. Soon the bitterness began to affect her health. She was angry, bitter and felt betrayed by the love of her life. He had exposed her and their child to the danger when he was supposed to be their protector. After sometime of leaving with the pain of unforgiveness, and seeing what this was doing to her as well, she chose to trust the Lord and stayed with her husband. She took a decision to rather forgive him as the bitterness was weighing heavily on her and affecting her health and the peace in the home.

After accepting her husband's condition and having forgiven him, she decided to do the tests and although she made these on several occasions, voluntarily and work-based testing, all the results came back negative. She took the child for testing and he also tested negative. Whilst there has been scientific proof of couples one being positive while the other negative, she was neither a carrier nor positive.

Years later she decided to add another child through normal means after she was counselled and prayed for. God in His mercy and wisdom blessed them with another child who also was negative although the husband remained positive.

Testimony 4

"If your enemy is hungry, give him bread to eat; and if he is thirsty, give him water to drink; for so you will heap coals of fire *on his head, and the Lord will reward you". Proverbs 25:21-22*

A beautiful woman, Christine comes from Limpopo and had met her husband, gotten married to him soon after that. He met her with a child, whom he promised to love and raise as his own. A year later, they were blessed with a son who was his first biological child. He was very excited and became a great father to his own blood and flesh. Two years later, they had another child and soon after this, things took a different turn.

He first started by rejecting his step son and then got the other children to reject him. They made him an outcast in his father's house. The other children could not relate to their own blood and this tore the mother's heart. She was in a marriage; she loved her husband and equally loved her son. Christine, made a decision to move the child away to stay with his grandmother as the other children had also started following in their father's footsteps and treated their brother as an outcast. Not long after, the husband refused the young man the visiting rights. He was no longer allowed to come to the family home or interact with his brothers. The man no longer hid his disgust and utter dislike of the young man.

To rub salt to the wounds, the mother-in-law also disliked her makoti. She was made to feel like an outcast, a reject by the family she was married into. The family was highly educated and they despised the act that she was not as educated as their son and the other makotis. He would always rub it in so that she knows he was educated while she came short. The fact that her husband listened and executed everything that his mother said made her life a living hell. His mother did not approve of their marriage and convinced him that Christine was not good enough for him.

Christine was raised from a good Christian family where she was taught good moral values. She was taught to love and had nothing but respect for her husband and her in-laws. Despite the opinion and perception of her mother in-law, she did everything she could to be a good loving wife and a good mother to her children. This teaching came very handy in her marriage. When the going was tough, she would retreat to her space and found solace in the Lord whom her mother believed in. She never stopped loving her husband and honoring her in laws despite the hatred and the treatment.

Unfortunately, even though she remained loyal to him, he started to demean her and began to cheat on her. He didn't hide it and made his love affairs with other women known to her and their education standard. This had a huge impact on her person, her self-confidence dipped. She was shadow of her former self. Her health also suffered and began to deteriorate. She became bitter, angry and wanted out of the marriage.

It was at this time that the husband began to be sick and was in and out of hospital. He contracted HIV from one of his many adulterous relationships. She only knew about this later after finding the results hidden in their bedroom. By that time, they were no longer sharing the bed as the relationship had soured.

She nursed him back to full health though. Her children loved their father and she loved her husband even though he had treated her badly. Seeing him pale and weak in the hospital broke her heart. Although she felt he somehow deserved it, she knew that it was not for her to revenge. Often, she had thought of leaving him while he was sick however this kind of thinking and attitude was foreign to her. She was raised differently with compassion.

Her pain was real. The hurt, the insults and the humiliations were all real. Anger, bitterness and unforgiveness were eating away her happiness. She was no longer the Christine she was before. She couldn't take the pressure anymore; the pain she felt was intense. She shad a very low esteem and started to isolate herself from the world around her. Often, she would park her car beside the road and be lost in deep thoughts. She wanted him to suffer and even die but at the same time, she wanted him to live.

During one of her visits to the hospital, she held his hand while he was asleep and began to pray for his recovery. Unknown to her, he was half asleep and could hear every word she was saying. She prayed from the bottom of her heart and meant every word. By God's grace, the husband was discharged from the hospital few days after that. He didn't live long but succumbed to the sickness sometime after being re-admitted.

Christine took a decision to put it in her own words,

"REMOE THE DEAD ROMAN FROM MY BACK". By this she meant to remove the heavy load she had been carrying of bitterness, anger and unforgiveness. She couldn't walk around carrying a dead roman on her back anymore; she needed to let it all go, the anger, the grudge, the resentment, the bitterness that was slowly consuming her. She said she came to realize that no amount of hatred will change her situation and that the only person who seems to suffer from this was her. She was tired of the load and knew that if she doesn't release the dead roman on her back, it will slowly kill her. She was weary of its impact and wanted out. She chose to live; she chose unconditional forgiveness.

To hate her husband would not resolve anything. It would not liberate her nor restore her dignity. She had concluded to forgive him regardless for her own sake.

It was this gesture, this decision that also melted his heart. He confessed that he had listened to her mother who influenced him against her. His relationship with his mother had also suffered as a result since he came out of hospital. He was now seeing his wife for what she was, a good woman he had decided to marry those many years ago. He had finally come to his senses but unfortunately it was too late.

Christine could have chosen to remain bitter, angry and never forgave her husband and the in-laws for all the bad treatment however that would not have solved anything. She chose to forgive and this impacted the whole family. Today she lives happily with her children and in good terms with her in-laws. Even her mother in-law came around and patched things with her. Glory to the Lord!

Part 5

Conclusions

Words are powerful

"Remind them of these things, charging them before the Lord not to strive about words to no profit, to the ruin of the hearers" 2 Timothy 2:14

Our Father used words to bring forth creation into existence. He spoke of things as if they are even though they were not and yet they became (Romans 4:17). This capacity is inherent to us since we are created in His image and likeness. One does not have to be a Christian to exercise this ability; it is a nature and capacity that exist within each human being. Anyone can exercise this at will. Scripture reminds us that the power of life and death lies in our tongues and those who love it will eat its fruits (Proverbs 18:21).

This means, while capacity and ability has been given to us, we should however understand and be ready for the aftermath of our words. For this reason, it is absolutely critical that we watch our mouths in our daily communications with any person even if they are not our relations. Words have devastating effects and once released cannot be taken back. They possess within them the creative power to bring forth anything.

Case Study 1

"Death and life are in the power of the tongue, and those who love it will eat its fruit" Proverbs 18:21

I heard of a man who lost his family many years ago after he spoke words he should not have spoken. He is a servant of the Lord who has been called into ministry. He was passionate about his calling but his wife kept dragging her feet and thus affecting his ministry. Being a married man, he didn't want to leave his wife behind but wanted her to be part of what God was doing in his life.

She had a tendency to delay him both in his assignment and when going for church services. In anger and frustrations, he told her that he wished the Lord would take her so that he may be free to do the work of ministry without anyone delaying him and thus holding him back on the assignment. A week later while travelling in a taxi, she was involved in an accident and died together with their only child. The man was devasted. Although he spoke the words yet he did not mean it to happen. Unfortunately, those words were fulfilled and he ate of the fruits of his mouth.

Case Study 2

"Where the word of a king is, there is power..."
Ecclesiastes 8:4

The next story is painful because the couple is known to me. A certain woman was fighting with her husband. She had requested him to take their child to school on his way to his meeting, but the husband refused. Earlier in the week, the wife had decided to take their child out of a school where she was attending to another school. The couple had discussed the matter and the husband refused the changes due to the financial implications.

The tuition fee was expensive and would bring an unnecessary stress on the family finances. In addition to the fees, the school was also far from his route of work which would have added extra expenses on the petrol. The husband had tried to reason with her but she refused to see reason and insisted on changing the child without his permission. The matter brought a lot of stress to their marriage. The husband had indicated that he wants nothing to do with the new school and that he was never going to be involved in anything to do with the new arrangements.

On this particular day, she insisted that he drop the child despite his position on the matter. When he refused, she burst in anger and tore the clothes he was wearing because they were bought by her. He was already late for an urgent meeting that morning at his work place and could not afford to be late. Out of anger, he reacted and not responded to the situation. He looked at his wife and spoke with authority, „you will never find peace in your life and went to change the torn clothes and left for work. After some time, she was involved in an accident and passed away. Like the first man, he also ate the fruits of the words of his mouth.

Case Study 3

It is critical that despite the disagreements, arguments and fighting, that level heads must prevail at all times. The authority given to man is far greater than we could ever imagine. We carry within us, our Father's abilities and creative capacity. The Lord Jesus warned us of this in his address and rebuke of the sons of Zebedee.

"Now it came to pass, when the time had come for Him to be received up, that He steadfastly set His face to go to Jerusalem, and sent messengers before His face. And as they went, they entered a village of the Samaritans, to prepare for Him. But they did not receive Him, because His face was set for the journey to Jerusalem. And when His disciples James and John saw this, they said,

> *"Lord, do You want us to command fire to come down from heaven and consume them, just as Elijah did?" But He turned and rebuked them, and said, „You do not know what manner of spirit you are of. For the Son of Man did not come to destroy men's lives but to save them" (Luke 9:51-55).*

Both James and John felt justified to take this action. The Lord Jesus had done a lot for the people and they felt the Samaritans were being spiteful, disrespectful and wanted to teach them a lesson they wouldn't forget. This is the attitude of most if not all of us when confronted with situations that undermine our reputations, ego and authority. We want to get even but, in the process, we forget that we are here as ambassadors of Christ. He came to save people's lives and not destroy them. As His disciples, we are to advance this agenda at all costs; therefore we must try our level best by His grace to safeguard the lives of people not to destroy them. We must forgive one another! It is not a request but a command. We are commanded to forgive.

"If you forgive the sins of any, they are forgiven them; if you retain the sins of any, they are retained" John 20:23

This is a huge load of responsibilities to humanity. We have the power to forgive or retain the sins and we must try our level best to forgive. Our Lord has set an example for us. On the cross, He could have asked the Father to avenge Him, seeing that He was innocent of all their accusations; however He chose to look beyond our current circumstances. He forgave us and asked the Father to do the same.

It is not enough to forgive but we have to go a step further and ask the Father to forgive them as well. The tangible measure of forgiveness is whether we are able to pray for our enemies. If we can, then we have truly forgiven them but if we are unable to open our mouth and say good things on their behalf before our Father, then we are still far from forgiveness. Our Lord Jesus did and asked the Father to forgive us. Let us follow His example.

Admonition

If you are struggling with bitterness, perhaps due to unfortunate incidents in your life and are willing to break loose from this bondage, I urge you to make this prayer with me. Our Father is a gracious loving God and He is waiting for this commitment to wipe your slate clean.

> *"Come now, and let us reason together," says the Lord, "though your sins are like scarlet, they shall be as white as snow; though they are red like crimson, they shall be as wool. If you are willing and obedient, you shall eat the good of the land" Isaiah 1:18-19.*

Say our Father who art in Heaven, I humble myself before You. I acknowledge my sin of un-forgiveness before You and cast my burdens unto You, in the name of Jesus Christ. I ask that you remove this yoke from me which is heavy and give me your yoke instead for it is light. Remove this burden from my shoulder and the yoke from my neck, destroying them with your anointing. Set me free that I may be free indeed according to your word and fill me with your Holy Spirit.

I reject any feeling of bitterness, hatred, envy and jealousy and I ask you to shut any door that might have been opened through these works of the flesh. Purify me and sanctify me with the blood of Jesus Christ that I may be renewed in the spirit of my mind. I pray Father that you may heal my soul and remove all the scars caused by un-forgiveness. If it pleases you Father, I also pray that you may wipe away every memory of bitterness, anger and un-forgiveness within me. I ask all these in the name of your Son, my Lord and Savior Jesus Christ the king.

About the Author

An ordained Apostle, Matlou Selepe is the senior pastor of Kingdom Impact Apostolic Centre aka KIAC which is based in Wesfort, Pretoria West. As a teacher of the word, his passion lies with the body of Christ's readiness for the second coming of the King. He loves spending time interceding for the church. It is from this premise that he wrote this book, believing that unforgiveness remains one of the stumbling blocks against spiritual growth in the body of Christ. He believes that the church holds the key to the second coming of the King and therefore must be ready and prepared for His coming lest she becomes the foolish virgin.

Pastor Matlou Selepe has authored four (4) books namely, Understanding the Gift of Tongues, The Truth Regarding Ancestral Worship, Understanding the Role of Baptism as well as The Case of True Salvation.

To contact Apostle Matlou Selepe

Email: selepemj@telkomsa.net
Contact: (+27) 082 442 0049

Reference

1. Stanley, Charles Dr., In Touch Daily Devotional, Friday 2006/10/07

2. Nemaungani, Rudzani Pastor, Christ Redeemer Church International, Marriage Counseling session, 2007

3. Dube, Lucky, Different Colors/One people,

   Victims,

Shanachie Records, 1993

5. Prince, Derek, The Grace of Yielding, Whitaker House, 1977

6. Joyner, Rick, The Final Quest, Morningstar Publications, 1996

7. Wegerle, Tony, Demons and Angels, Christian Life, 1990, 2001.